Hard Knocks

Hard Knocks

A LIFE STORY OF THE VANISHING WEST

BY HARRY ("SAM") YOUNG

with an Introduction by James D. McLaird

SOUTH DAKOTA STATE HISTORICAL SOCIETY PRESS

Pierre, South Dakota

The text of *Hard Knocks: A Life Story of the Vanishing West* is reproduced from the edition
published in 1915 by the J. K. Gill Company and Wells & Company of Portland, Oreg.

This publication is funded, in part, by the
Deadwood Publications Fund provided by the City of Deadwood
and the Deadwood Historic Preservation Commission.

Library of Congress Cataloging-in-Publication Data
Young, Harry, 1849-1940.
Hard knocks : a life story of the vanishing West / by Harry "Sam" Young ;
with an introduction by James D. McLaird.
p. cm.
Originally published: Portland, Or. : J.K. Gill Co., 1915.
Includes bibliographical references and index. ISBN 0-9749195-1-9
1. Young, Harry, 1849-1940. 2. Young, Harry, 1849-1940—Childhood and youth. 3.
Pioneers—West (U.S.)—Biography. 4. Frontier and pioneer life—West (U.S.) 5. West
(U.S.)—Biography. 6. West (U.S.)—Social life and customs—19th century. I. Title.
F594.Y72 2005
978'.02'092—dc22   [B]

ISBN 0-9749195-1-9
Printed in the United States of America
10 09 08 07 06 05   1 2 3 4 5

Frontispiece and cover: Harry ("Sam") Young
Cover insert: The Shooting of Wild Bill Hickok, 1940, oil on canvas, by artist William Lackey

DEDICATION

To those brave and generous men whom

I met and knew along the rugged Life Journey herein described,

I dedicate these treasures of a fruitful memory. May those who

fell by the wayside rest peacefully, and those who still trudge on,

find Life's Trail less difficult as they approach its end.

Harry Young

ORIGINAL PUBLISHER'S NOTE

In presenting this book, the publishers feel that they need not emphasize either its purpose or its merits. They will speak for themselves. The reader will need no spur to his interest, nor the work require either apology or explanation. Interest is certain from beginning to end, and few readers will wish to lay the book aside until they have reached the end of the rapidly succeeding incidents. If crudity mar in any respect, it will be quickly forgotten in the manifest truthfulness and candor of the narrator.

The great lesson of the book is that "truth is stranger than fiction." The life story here given belongs to a generation that has not only seen the world's greatest advancement, but has been a part of the greatest development of our own country. It has been a period rich in story, and the experiences here detailed run like a thread through the entire fabric. In the main, they deal not with the great heroes,—the Carsons, the Custers, and the Buffalo Bills,—but with the great multitude of brave and adventurous spirits that have swept over the West in the past generation, and to whose undaunted courage and tireless energy our development is mainly due.

CONTENTS

INTRODUCTION

James D. McLaird

ONLY three weeks after Jack McCall murdered James Butler ("Wild Bill") Hickok in Mann and Lewis's Saloon No. 10 on 2 August 1876, bartender Harry ("Sam") Young shot and killed Myer ("Bummer Dan") Baum in the same establishment. It was a bizarre incident. Young and a local gambler named Samuel ("Laughing Sam") Hartman had been quarreling for several weeks. During that time, Hartman repeatedly threatened to kill Young, once even asking Carl Mann, owner of the saloon, to loan him his pistol for that purpose. Mann warned Hartman that such an action would have serious consequences. Nonetheless, on the evening of 22 August, a determined Hartman entered the building where Young was working. Simultaneously, Hartman's friend, Myer Baum, who for some reason was wearing Hartman's coat, walked through the saloon. Assuming the man in the coat was Hartman, Young immediately fired. According to the local newspaper, when Young surrendered to the authorities he told them "that he thought he had shot the wrong man."[1]

At Young's trial, defense lawyers insisted that the shooting was an act of self-defense. In their view, Hartman's repeated threats against Young had forced him to react instantly when the man he assumed was Hartman approached. The jury agreed, finding Young not guilty. The local editor, in a clear reference to the fact that Jack McCall had also been found not guilty after he shot

Hickok, commented cynically that the jury "after 3 1/2 hours de-
liberation returned the usual verdict."[2]

Interestingly, Sam Young did not mention his shooting of
Baum in his memoir, *Hard Knocks: A Life Story of the Vanishing West*
(1915).[3] Instead, Young's account of his adventures during the
Black Hills gold rush ends abruptly with his departure from
Deadwood on 1 October 1876 (p. 231). It is possible he omitted the
incident because he feared legal repercussions. After all, Jack
McCall had been retried, declared guilty, and executed in Yankton
after Deadwood's 1876 court decision was determined not to be
binding because the region did not have territorial status at the
time.[4] Or, Young may have left the shooting out of his memoir
simply to avoid personal embarrassment. Whatever his motive,
Young's failure to relate his shooting of Baum is supremely ironic
in light of his intention to impress readers of *Hard Knocks* with the
lawless conditions that prevailed during the frontier period.

According to his own account, Young was only fourteen in 1863
when, inspired by his childhood reading of dime novels, he ran
away from his home in New York State to go west. On the frontier,
he hoped to replicate the adventures of his fictional heroes and
"assist in the extermination of the Noble Red Man" (p. 9). Although he never completely abandoned his youthful dreams, actual conditions in the West often challenged Young's dime-novel
notions. For example, at Fort Smith, Arkansas, the young runaway met a trapper named "Kentuck Hugh" who, he thought, resembled his fictional heroes. Young was excited at Hugh's invita-
tion to join him on his trek to Fort Gibson, 125 miles northwest of
Fort Smith. Rather than experiencing romantic adventures, how-

ever, Young found himself begging and stealing to get food for his companion and himself. In addition, the first American Indian the pair met spoke English and invited them to dinner. Hugh later deserted Young, leaving him to fend for himself (pp. 13-21).

Young's dime-novel romanticism and naiveté about conditions in the West led new acquaintances to tease him in inventive ways. For example, when Young found work with a railroad surveying crew, his companions had their Indian guide disguise himself, whoop loudly, and take Young captive (pp. 28-29). On another occasion, Young awakened to find what he thought was a snake crawling in his blankets, only to discover that the snake was a wiggling cattail held by one of his friends (pp. 26-27). Despite these disillusionments, Young sometimes experienced the West as he imagined it.

Meeting Wild Bill Hickok was one of the highlights of his travels. Because of his predisposition, Young believed the exaggerated tales then circulating about the gunfighter's legendary feats. In fact, he even added to them. It was in Hays City, Kansas, in 1868, Young says, that he first met Hickok, then serving as the town's law officer. According to Young, Hickok advised him to spend less time in saloons and dance halls and even helped him find work (pp. 41-42). Although his story cannot be substantiated, it may be true. Young's fanciful tales about Hickok's shootings in Kansas, however, are demonstrably false. For example, he repeats popular accounts that in earlier years Hickok had killed nine members of the "McCanless gang" in a bloody battle. Then, Young adds, Hickok shot seven soldiers in Hays City, two of them by firing over his shoulder, twenty-five men in

Abilene, and nine more in Ellsworth in order to bring peace to these communities (pp. 44-52). In actuality, asserts Hickok biographer Joseph G. Rosa, there were only four people in the McCanles party, and one of them was a boy. Of this group, Hickok is "credited" with killing, at most, only three men. And, Rosa adds, Hickok probably killed only seven men in his entire career.[5]

Bibliographer Ramon F. Adams discovered further errors in Young's account of Hickok. For example, Young claims that the first man Hickok killed was David Tutt in 1865 (pp. 43-44); however, Hickok's fight with McCanles had actually occurred four years earlier. In Young's account of Hickok killing twenty-five men in Abilene (he actually killed only two), he failed to mention that Hickok accidently shot his own deputy. This incident occurred during a fracas in which Hickok killed Phil Coe (Young misspells his name as Cole). In addition, Young claims that Hickok met and married Mrs. Lake in Kansas City in the 1860s, whereas Hickok did not marry Agnes Lake until 1876 in Cheyenne.[6]

Because of these mistakes and Young's "wild tales of wholesale blood-letting," some historians have dismissed Young's memoirs as unreliable.[7] Calamity Jane biographer Roberta Beed Sollid went so far as to denounce Young as an "imposter." She asserted that Young "wrote as if he were an eye-witness to every event that took place in the Black Hills" but that in the documents she examined he was unmentioned. She especially doubted that Young was an eyewitness to the shooting of Wild Bill Hickok. "It is common knowledge among Deadwood citizens," Sollid claimed, "that Anson Tippie was the bartender at the fatal shooting of Hickok," not Young.[8] Sollid might have been less hostile had she been aware of Young's shooting of Baum, which proves that he was indeed a bartender in Saloon No. 10 in August 1876. Furthermore, the *Chicago Inter-Ocean*, reporting on the killing of Hickok and the trial of McCall, summarized Sam Young's testimony at the trial. The journalist noted that Young "was engaged in the saloon," owned by Mann and Lewis, and testified that he "had just delivered $15 worth of pocket checks to the deceased" when he heard McCall cry out, "Take that," as he fired.[9]

Other evidence that Sollid missed also proves that Young was in the region at this time. For example, Young says that before he went to the Black Hills he worked for John Hunton, who ran a road ranch between Cheyenne and Fort Laramie (pp. 181-82). Hunton kept detailed records, including a daily account of events at his stopping place. Young is listed in Hunton's 1874-1875 ledger, which indicates that at that time Hunton owed Young forty-four dollars.[10] Not only that, some of Young's most outlandish tales can be shown to be genuine. In one story, for example, Young tells about a "Mexican" who cut off an Indian's head to claim a reward offered in Deadwood for scalps when fear of Indians was at its peak in 1876. Afterwards, Young says, he joined Calamity Jane and others who paraded with the head through the streets, finishing the celebration with their version of a "war dance" (pp. 211-12). A contemporary newspaper verifies that this disgusting event actually occurred.[11] Young tells another unusual story that happened in Custer. There, Tom Milligan and his partner, after imbibing heavily at the town's saloon, decided to shoot targets in the street. Somehow, the drunken Milligan managed to shoot his

partner in the head (pp. 189-91). The 24 March 1876 Yankton
newspaper confirms that this event actually occurred, noting that
although Milligan had shot and killed his partner, Alec Shaw, he
had only been fined for shooting within the city limits.[12]

Unlike later historians, Young's contemporaries believed his
stories were authentic. Writers seeking information about the
early West frequently consulted him. Among those who visited
Young before his death was Joe E. Milner, son of scout Moses
("California Joe") Milner who had guided the 1875 Walter P.
Jenney Expedition to the Black Hills. California Joe had also been
a personal friend of Hickok's. At Milner's request, Young described the saloon in which Hickok was killed and provided details about Wild Bill's death. Milner used these details in his book
California Joe (1935).[13] Another book that borrowed heavily from
Young was *McGillycuddy Agent* (1941), which recounted the story
of Valentine T. McGillycuddy, topographer for the Jenney Expedition. McGillycuddy's account of Calamity Jane is largely derived
from Young's narrative.[14]

Thus, although Young's account must be used cautiously because it contains exaggerations and errors, his story includes
much information of value to historians. For example, Young's
stories about Calamity Jane accompanying the Jenney Expedition
to the Black Hills in 1875 are accurate. Dispatches sent by newspaper correspondents with the expedition confirm that she followed the troops escorting the Jenney party into the Hills.[15] Likewise, Young's claim that Calamity Jane worked for Al Swearingen,
owner of what became known as the Gem Theater, Deadwood's
most popular dance hall, is supported by other witnesses.[16] Jour-

nalist Leander Richardson, who camped with Hickok in July 1876, even suggests that Calamity "bossed a dancehouse" of her own that summer,[17] perhaps confirming Young's assertion that she was in charge of the women at Swearingen's place (p. 206). Because these early sources support Young's stories about Calamity's activities in 1875 and 1876, his personal anecdotes about her riding in his wagon during the Jenney Expedition (pp. 170-72) and about her recruiting girls for Swearingen's dance hall (pp. 205-6) seem credible, as well.

Young's description of the shooting of Wild Bill, as stated earlier, is also drawn from personal observation. In *Hard Knocks*, Young records that Hickok's murderer, Jack McCall, ran from the saloon and mounted a horse to escape. However, McCall fell to the ground because the horse's cinch was loose, leading to the shooter's capture by the pursuing crowd. Young's version of McCall's bungled escape is confirmed by another witness,[18] although in her autobiography, published in 1896, Calamity Jane claims that she personally cornered McCall in a butcher shop.[19] Even though Young repeated some popular tales about Calamity Jane and Wild Bill, here he gives credit for the assassin's capture to Tom Mulquinn, who grabbed McCall from behind as the crowd closed in (p. 221). In this case, Young stuck to the facts as he knew them.

Despite the evidence supporting Young's veracity, the attacks on his credibility by historians are understandable. Young himself opened the door to criticism by carelessly misspelling names and misplacing events. A few inaccuracies are merely typographical or spelling errors by a person who is spelling "by ear":

Bill Nuttall becomes Bill Nuttle or Al Swearingen becomes Al
Swarringer, for example. More curious is Young's reference to the
saloon owned by Carl Mann as Saloon No. 66 (p. 196); all other
sources refer to it as No. 10. Whether this error is a result of his
faulty memory or whether the saloon was once called No. 66 cannot be determined, but Young correctly documents the saloon's
ownership. He notes that Bill Nuttall built the place and Carl
Mann and Jerry Lewis bought the establishment from him (p.
196). The change of ownership can be traced in early newspaper
accounts that refer to it first as Nuttall and Mann's and then Mann
and Lewis's saloon.[20] Most of Young's errors result from his rely-
ing solely on memory. Abilene's first marshal was Bear River
Smith, not Green River Smith; and the first mayor of Custer was
Joseph G. Bemis not E. B. Farnum (Farnum was actually
Deadwood's first mayor). Cloudy recollections later in life also
affected Young's chronology. In his account, for example, Abilene
is founded in 1869 with Hickok as sheriff; in reality, Abilene was
established in 1867, and Hickok did not become its chief law
officer until 1871. Thus, Young could not have met Hickok there in
1869 as he claims.

More serious errors occur in Young's version of Calamity
Jane's origins. In his account, Calamity Jane is born Jane Dalton
at Fort Laramie in 1860 and nicknamed "Calamity" after her parents are killed by Indians. The soldiers at Fort Laramie adopted
her, Young says, leading to her unusual dress and behavior (pp.
169-70). But contemporary documents and her own autobiography show that Calamity Jane's given name was Martha Canary, and
she was born in Princeton, Missouri, in 1856. She probably only

arrived in the Fort Laramie area about 1873-1874.[21] Although
Young may be excused for his errors about Calamity Jane's birth
since he might have heard this version while in the West, it is not
easy to forgive him for intentional distortions designed to ro-
manticize the old West. In *Hard Knocks*, for example, he changes
the date of Calamity Jane's death from 1 August 1903 to 2 August
1906 in order to claim that she died "on the same day and month,
and the same hour, Wild Bill was assassinated thirty years before"
(pp. 206-7).

But all recollections contain errors, and for readers, the final
question is whether Young's mistakes outweigh his contribu-
tions. What remains after the mistakes, exaggerations, and tall
tales are removed from Young's recollections? The answer is an
interesting narrative about a young man who ran away from home
to experience firsthand the adventures he had read about in dime
novels. In his quest, Young traveled through Arkansas, Oklahoma, Kansas, Colorado, Wyoming, Dakota, Utah, Nevada, California, Oregon, and Alaska. He actually met some of his heroes,
such as Wild Bill Hickok, and experienced gold rushes, railroad
booms, homesteading, and cowboy life. Even though Young did
not record his youthful experiences until he was in his sixties, in
Hard Knocks he nevertheless managed to convey his feelings as a
teenager and young adult alone in the West. Young mostly relates
personal anecdotes rather than describes how the West was
settled. He is unabashedly honest about his saloon escapades and
relationships with dance hall girls. In fact, for Young, "the dance
hall girl was the true pioneer woman of the West" (p. 67).

Most importantly, Young helps fill a void in personal reminis-

cences about the pioneer West. Although numerous accounts
have been written by travelers, journalists, town builders, home-
steaders, and ranchers, only a few common laborers penned their
stories. Harry ("Sam") Young is one of those ordinary people who
did. Besides bartending, he worked as cattle herder, buffalo skinner, night watchman, and general handyman in the West. Once,
he even dug potatoes for a farmer to pay his expenses. But his pri-
mary occupation was that of teamster. Young usually hauled supplies for the military, but he also worked in this capacity for other
government entities. In 1875, he drove "lead wagon" for the
Jenney Expedition to the Black Hills. To be given the position at
the front, Young claims, was prestigious; it meant he carried the
equipment of Colonel Richard Dodge, commander of the military
escort (pp. 154-55). It was the highest honor Young received as a
teamster. More often, he found himself in trouble with the military. He complains bitterly about dictatorial post commanders,
especially young West Pointers who severely disciplined even ci-
vilian workers (pp. 161-65). Young, who admits to having a short
temper, was finally "black-balled" for disobeying orders, making
it nearly impossible for him to gain further employment at military posts (pp. 185-86).

Young's recollections also include his impressions of life and
work at Red Cloud Agency. For a while, Young was in charge of
driving cattle to the agency, and he provides a firsthand account
of the distribution of beef and annuities to the Lakotas, or western Sioux (pp. 127-30). Young's description of conditions at Red
Cloud and his comments about the Indians are written from the
perspective of a nineteenth-century working man. Consequently,

his account lacks sophistication and shares the prejudices of his era. According to Young, during the time he worked at the agency the government's policy was to "civilize" the Indians through kindness.[22] Nevertheless, Young's account of agency life emphasizes conflicts between the Sioux and agency employees. The most serious incident led to the murder of Frank Appleton, the son of the agency's "boss farmer" (pp. 149-52). In Young's opinion, this event caused the government to move Indian affairs from the Interior Department to the War Department and precipitated the Sioux war of 1876.[23]

Details about Young's life after he left the northern plains in 1876 are sketchy. Mostly he worked around Portland, Oregon, in jobs related to transportation. In 1879, for example, he was in charge of supplying Northern Pacific construction crews with food and other necessities (pp. 235-36). Later, he became manager of the Baggage & Omnibus Transfer Company, then served as traveling passenger agent for the Union Pacific Railway Company. When he retired in 1922, he was working for the Pacific Steamship Company. Following his death in November 1925, the Portland *Oregonian* noted that Young was survived by "his widow" and a son, who was then living in the Belgian Congo. Unfortunately, the article provided no other details about his immediate family. The newspaper did, however, mention that he had two brothers and two sisters living in Canada and a brother-in-law, Joseph W. Beveridge, residing in Oregon.[24]

Even before Young's death, his book *Hard Knocks* was out of print. The first edition, a second edition, and a possible third, all published in Portland in 1915, sold out quickly. Another edition, printed in Chicago, quickly followed suit. Since then, *Hard Knocks* has only been available from libraries and out-of-print book dealers. In a review of different copies of the book, four distinct bindings and at least three printings can be identified. The first edition, which was a limited press run, appears to have been bound in green-marbled, paper-covered boards with a brown cloth spine with black lettering.[25] The book contained an errata notice printed on the final page that corrected an error in distance on page 13 and an errata slip pasted to page 68 that corrected the spelling of Bat Masterson's name. The second edition corrected these errors within the text and appeared in two bindings: one a deluxe edition of red cloth with gilt lettering; the other of red cloth with black lettering. The title page of the gilt edition carries an extra line in an unmatched typeface, attributing the publication to "The J. K. Gill Company" (this version could represent a new binding of previously printed sheets or a third printing as well as a third binding). Each of these Portland editions or binding states contains twenty-five plates, some of which are crude sketches while others are photographs. The Chicago edition, published by Laird and Lee, is printed on cheaper paper in brown cloth with black lettering. It contains only seventeen plates but features a dust jacket bearing Wild Bill Hickok's portrait. All the later printings appear to reproduce the same, corrected text.

    The text of this 2005 edition is a facsimile of the J. K. Gill Company printing. The frontispiece of the author and the drawing of Hickok's murder, which shows Young himself near the card table, are reproduced from the original plates. The other plates have been replaced with a selection of photographs of the same or similar subjects from archival collections.

In 1915, Sam Young's adventures and his book tapped into the American longing for a romanticized past. The Portland *Oregonian* reported on the book's initial appearance that *Hard Knocks* "is a dramatic rehearsal of incidents compiled from the stirring days when the West was young." Suspecting that aspects of the book were exaggerated, the reviewer nevertheless noted that Young relied on his "personal experiences and those of his friends," calling up memories and portraying people "so that they cannot be mistaken" in identity.[26] In spite of his occasional legend building and inaccuracies, Young had served up a gritty portrait of the workingman's frontier in *Hard Knocks*, one that still captures the interest and imagination of modern readers.

NOTES

1. *Black Hills Pioneer*, 26 Aug. 1876.

2. Ibid.

3. Harry ("Sam") Young, *Hard Knocks: A Life Story of the Vanishing West* (Portland, Oreg.: Wells & Co., 1915). The numbers in the text refer to the reprint edition of the book that follows this Introduction.

4. Joseph G. Rosa, *They Called Him Wild Bill: The Life and Adventures of James Butler Hickok*, 2d ed., rev. (Norman: University of Oklahoma Press, 1974), pp. 318-37. *See also* Rosa's *Jack McCall, Assassin: An Updated Account of His Yankton Trial, Plea for Clemency, and Execution* (n.p.: English Westerners Society, 1998).

5. Rosa, *They Called Him Wild Bill*, pp. 4, 45-52.

6. Adams, *Burs under the Saddle: A Second Look at Books and Histories of the West* (Norman: University of Oklahoma Press, 1964), pp. 577-79.

7. Ibid., p. 578. Likewise, historian J. Leonard Jennewein called *Hard Knocks* "a free-wheeling book, filled with action, anecdote, and error" (Jennewein, *Black Hills Booktrails* [Mitchell, S.Dak.: Dakota Territory Centennial Commission & Dakota Wesleyan Unversity, 1962], p. 37).

8. Sollid, *Calamity Jane: A Study in Historical Criticism* (1958; reprint ed., Helena: Montana Historical Society Press, 1995), p. 7. Sollid's assertion that Anson Tippie, not Sam Young, was bartender in Saloon No. 10 seems to derive from statements either by Tippie himself or by John S. McClintock, who credits his account of Hickok's death to Tippie, "the bartender in the saloon where [Hickok] was killed, who witnessed the affair" (McClintock, *Pioneer Days in the Black Hills: Accurate History and Facts Related by One of the Early Day Pioneers* [Deadwood, S.Dak.: By the Author, 1939], p. 108). Interestingly, McClintock's introduction of Tippie does not contradict Young's account; Young himself records a second bartender at the No. 10 on the morning of 2 August. Young came on watch that morning, "relieving the night man" who told him that Hickok and the card players had been at it all night (p. 219). While the second man may still have been present later in the day, it is clear that Young was on duty at the time of the shooting because he was the bartender called to testify at McCall's Deadwood trial. *Chicago Inter-Ocean*, 17 Aug. 1876.

9. *Chicago Inter-Ocean*, 17 Aug. 1876. Newspaper accounts of Black Hills events frequently appear in sources far removed from the region. In the nineteenth century, before syndicated news, local residents often served as correspondents for newspapers located elsewhere. The *Inter-Ocean* article, for example, bears the dateline "Special Correspondence

of the Inter-Ocean, Deadwood, D.T., Aug. 3, 1876." Black Hills news items were also frequently reprinted in other newspapers. The Yankton newspaper, for example, regularly devoted columns to the Black Hills to satisfy the curiosity of local readers. This broad dissemination of news is fortunate because many early Black Hills newspapers are no longer extant.

10. L. G. ["Pat"] Flannery, ed., *John Hunton's Diary, Volume 1, 1873-'75* (Fort Laramie, Wyo.: By the Editor, 1956), pp. 10, 33. *See also* William Francis Hooker, *The Bullwhacker: Adventures of a Frontier Freighter*, ed. Howard R. Driggs (Yonkers-on-Hudson, N.Y.: World Book Co., 1924), p. 163.

11. *Laramie Sentinel*, 2 Sept. 1876. The newspaper indicates that two similar incidents occurred only a few days apart; Young's account seems to blend the two events.

12. *Daily Press and Dakotaian* (Yankton, D.T.), 24 Mar. 1876.

13. Milner and Earle R. Forrest, *California Joe: Noted Scout and Indian Fighter* (Caldwell, Idaho: Caxton Printers, 1935), pp. 243, 253-56.

14. Julia B. McGillycuddy, *McGillycuddy Agent: A Biography of Dr. Valentine T. McGillycuddy* (Stanford University, Calif.: Stanford University Press, 1941), pp. 25-27, 33-34. McGillycuddy's wife put this book together from her husband's notes. For a textual comparison showing that McGillycuddy's story was derived from Young, *see* Sollid, *Calamity Jane*, pp. 5-9.

15. *Chicago Tribune*, 19 June 1875; *Daily Press and Dakotaian*, 6 July 1875. For more on the Jenney Expedition, *see* James D. McLaird and Lesta V. Turchen, "The Scientists' Search for Gold, 1875: Walter P. Jenney and Henry Newton," *South Dakota History* 4 (Fall 1974): 404-38.

16. When the Gem Theater burned down in 1899, the *Deadwood Daily*

Pioneer-Times, 20 Dec. 1899, reminisced that when E. A. ("Al") Swearingen started the business in 1876, "There were but three women available—Calamity Jane, Kitty Arnold and Mr. Swearingen's wife." The three women and a boy dressed as a woman sold wine to the patrons, according to this *Times* story that may have been based on an interview with Swearingen himself. Young's descriptions of Calamity Jane suggest that she mainly dressed and acted like a man, but other sources indicate that she made her living in the dance halls in female attire. Like Young, Joseph ("White Eye") Anderson, *I Buried Hickok: The Memoirs of White Eye Anderson,* ed. William B. Secrest (College Station, Tex.: Creative Publishing Co., 1980), p. 102, recorded that when she arrived in Deadwood in the summer of 1876 Calamity was clad only in buckskins. But Anderson goes on to say that members of Hickok's party contributed funds so that she could buy a dress in order to "do business." Several days later, she showed up in "female clothes" and repaid the loan. In subsequent years, Calamity Jane did not confine her activities to the Gem. Clement Lounsberry, editor of the *Bismarck Tribune*, reported that she was making her living in Deadwood dance halls, noting in his 17 August 1877 edition (possibly from personal experience with her as partner) that she "waltzes on one leg and polkas on the other."

17. Richardson, quoted in James D. McLaird, "'I Know . . . because I Was There': Leander P. Richardson Reports the Black Hills Gold Rush," in *Gold Rush: The Black Hills Story*, comp. John D. McDermott (Pierre: South Dakota State Historical Society Press, 2001), p. 66.

18. McClintock, *Pioneer Days in the Black Hills*, p. 108. *See also Black Hills Pioneer*, 5 Aug. 1876.

19. [Martha Canary], *Life and Adventures of Calamity Jane by Herself* (n.p., [1896]), pp. 4-5.

20. *Black Hills Pioneer*, 5, 26 Aug. 1876; *Chicago Inter-Ocean*, 17 Aug. 1876. The transfer of ownership occurred close to the time of Hickok's death. The correspondent for the *Chicago Inter-Ocean*, writing on 3 August, refers to "the saloon kept by Messrs. Lewis & Mann," while the local *Pioneer* still has it as "the hall of Nuttall & Mann" on the fifth. By 26 August, the *Pioneer* also refers to the No. 10 as being owned by "Messrs. Mann & Lewis."

21. Canary, *Life and Adventures of Calamity Jane*, p. 1; Richard W. Etulain, "Calamity Jane: The Making of a Frontier Legend," in *Wild Women of the Old West*, ed. Glenda Riley and Etulain (Golden, Colo.: Fulcrum Publishing, 2003), pp. 177-80.

22. For more information about the people of Red Cloud Agency in this era, *see* George E. Hyde, *Red Cloud's Folk: A History of the Oglala Indians* (1937; reprint ed., Norman: University of Oklahoma Press, 1987).

23. Young is in error about the impact of the Appleton murder; the change in the government's policy toward the Sioux occurred for other reasons. For more information, *see* John S. Gray, *Centennial Campaign: The Sioux War of 1876* (Norman: University of Oklahoma Press, 1988), pp. 23-34.

24. *Portland Oregonian*, 14 Nov. 1925.

25. Ibid., 17 Aug. 1915.

26. Ibid.

Although taken later (1883), this photograph shows many people that Young met as he traveled the West. Seated, from left: Charles Bassett, Wyatt Earp, Frank McLain, and Neal Brown. Standing, from left: W. H. Harris, Luke Short, W. B. ("Bat") Masterson, W. F. Petillon. Courtesy Ford County Historical Society, Dodge City, Kans.

Big Steve, left, Con Moyer, center, and Ace Moyer, right, were hanged in Laramie City in 1868 for a variety of crimes. Courtesy of Wyoming State Archives, Department of State Parks and Cultural Resources

James Butler ("Wild Bill") Hickok befriended Sam Young in Hayes City, Kansas. Young was the bartender at Saloon No. 10 when Hickok was killed in Deadwood, Dakota Territory. Courtesy South Dakota State Historical Society

*Working at Red Cloud Agency, Young met several famous
American Indians, including [left] Man Afraid of His Horses, Little Wound,
and [right] Red Cloud (Charles M. Bell photograph).
Courtesy South Dakota State Historical Society*

Young worked much of his life as a teamster, driving six-mule teams similar to this one. Courtesy South Dakota State Historical Society

California Joe was the guide for the 1875 Jenney Expedition to the Black Hills. Courtesy South Dakota State Historical Society

Calamity Jane, shown here during the Jenney Expedition, often rode with Young as he drove the lead wagon (A. Guerin photograph). Courtesy J. Leonard Jennewein Collection, Layne Library, Dakota Wesleyan University, Mitchell, S.Dak.

The Jenney Expedition met a party of miners prospecting for gold on Castle Creek in 1875 (A. Guerin photograph). Courtesy South Dakota State Historical Society

Deadwood bustled with activity during the gold rush days of 1876-1877. Courtesy South Dakota State Historical Society

Despite her rough-and-tumble reputation, Calamity Jane could also appear feminine and well-dressed. Courtesy South Dakota State Historical Society

Bartender Sam Young provided the description for this sketch of the shooting of Wild Bill Hickok (artist unknown).

*Sculptor J. H. Riordan erected monuments to Wild Bill Hickok
(Grabill photograph) and Henry Weston Smith (Locke & McBride photograph)
in 1891. Smith was an itinerant preacher who was killed after giving a sermon
in Deadwood in 1876. Courtesy South Dakota State Historical Society*

HARD KNOCKS

CHAPTER I.

A LIFE IN SUMMARY—EFFECTS OF DIME NOVEL LITER-
ATURE—A FOURTEEN-YEAR-OLD RUNAWAY—THE
LOST BROTHER—ALONE IN NEW YORK—OFF FOR
THE WESTERN PLAINS—MY STRANGE FRIEND,
"THE HEALER."

IN this country where blood and station count for
naught, and where the race of life is open to all
comers, it is for little more than a mere matter
of record to say that I, Harry Young, the author,
was born in Cape Vincent, New York, in 1849.
I left my home in 1863, at the age of 14 years, and,
as this narrative will show, have lived in the West
ever since that time. My home is now in Portland,
Oregon, the metropolis of the great Northwest. When
observation shows me what has been accomplished by
the people of this section (to the generation of which
it has been my privilege to belong), I feel a pardon-
able pride in the fact that it is in the midst of these
people my life thus far has been spent.

I am not sure that there was much, if any, patriot-
ism in my early sentiments, but there was certainly a
decided tinge of romance in my make-up, doubtless due
to my having stored in my brain a considerable amount
of literature of the dramatic variety. I had read
everything obtainable in the line of dime novels, and
my head was so filled with "hair-raising" stories of
Indians, hunters, trappers, and other denizens of the
Wild West, that I had my mind made up that it was
my duty to go forth and encroach upon the domains
of those nomads and assist in the extermination of the
Noble Red Man.

One beautiful morning I stole away from home and
boarded a vessel called the "Greyhound." I had taken

my departure without going through the formality of
bidding my parents good-bye, or even of obtaining
their consent. The "Greyhound" was bound for
Oswego, New York, and was loaded with shingle
bolts. The distance was short, and, after a two-days'
sail, we arrived at our destination. I worked for two
days helping unload the vessel, for which I received the
munificent sum of two dollars and fifty cents. This
was in "shinplasters,—the old money of war times. I
had never been away from home before for more than
two days at a time in my life, except to visit friends
and relatives.

With this two dollars and fifty cents snugly stowed
away in my pocket, I made my way to Fulton, New
York. I was aware before leaving home that my
brother "Bill," as we called him, was working in a machine shop there. I determined to find him if possible.
It was noon when I arrived in Fulton, and I went into
the first machine shop I saw. As I entered, on a lathe
lay a pair of greasy trousers which I recognized as a
part of "Bill's" old working clothes, although he had
been away from home for one year.

I sat down and waited for some of the men to come
back from their dinner. Presently, one of them
walked in and I asked him if "Bill" Young worked in
that shop.

"Yes," he replied, "he's here. You stay with those
old pants and you will find him soon, for they belong
to him."

Bill came in shortly afterward and was much surprised to see me. He immediately wanted to know
where I was going. I informed him that I was bound
for New York, but did not tell him it was my intention
to become an Indian fighter.

"You may stay here tonight," he said, "but in the
morning you must go back home. I know you have
run away."

I begged to be allowed to go on, and after a while he consented. The next morning he paid my fare to New York City. I have never seen him since.

I arrived in New York City that night at ten o'clock. I shall never forget it. I alighted at the old Hudson River depot, at Tenth Avenue and Thirtieth Street, and was carrying an old-style grip-sack. The hackmen immediately began to crowd around me, each urging me to ride with him. I did not care to do so as I now had but sixty-five cents in my pocket.

Presently, one of the hackmen snatched my carpet bag from my hand, and placing it on the seat of the vehicle, insisted on my getting in. I refused to do so, and told my troubles to a passing policeman. He compelled the hackman to give up my bag, and asked me where I wanted to go. On being informed that I was a stranger in the city wanting to find a cheap lodging house, he took me across the street to a place having a lunch counter on the ground floor and rooms upstairs. I was not hungry, and went to bed without supper.

Shortly after retiring, I was disturbed by something, I knew not what. I sprang up bewildered, lighted the candle, and turned down the bedding. Good heavens! My companions were there by the thousands. I went down and told the clerk that although I was fond of life and enjoyed it as much as anyone, there were times when there could be too much of it, especially in a bed. I sat up the balance of the night.

The next day I obtained a position as bell boy in the Weldon Hotel, at the corner of Broadway and Howard Streets. After working there for several months I went to New Orleans, from which place I worked my passage to Memphis on the old steamer "Bismark." From there I made my way to Fort Smith, Arkansas.

At Fort Smith I became acquainted with a queer character, the first of many whom I met later on in the course of my travels. This man was about sixty years old, fully six feet in height, with gray hair, long gray beard, and the longest arms and fingers I have ever seen on anyone. He took a great fancy to me and told me a great many strange things, among them, that he was "a healer" and could locate and cure any disease by the laying on of his hands. He said that he had just arrived in town, and wanted just such a boy as myself to sell tickets and distribute handbills for the public healing which he proposed to do while there. We finally arrived at an understanding and had some bills printed, which I distributed. These an- announced in glowing terms that "The Healer" would be at the hotel that evening at eight o'clock and would cure all ills that human flesh was heir to.

When the much anticipated hour arrived, the only persons present were five old women, one of whom was an old negro mammy, who had with her a humpbacked boy. She requested the heeler to remove the de- formity. The healer informed her that he could do so and asked her to return with the boy at ten o'clock on the following morning. She became indignant, saying she had paid ten cents and was entitled to an immediate cure. The other women agreed with her, which caused considerable commotion and terminated in the breaking up of the entertainment. (Total re- ceipts were sixty cents). Becoming thoroughly dis- gusted I went to bed, and shortly after was joined by my bedfellow, The Healer. For the remainder of the night, he kept me in a state of constant fear by talking to the spirits. I made a firm mental resolve then and there, that if good fortune permitted me to live until morning, I would dissolve partnership with my strange friend. Rising early, without disturbing him, I des- cended to the hotel office, and after some very rapid thinking, I concluded to leave the town before the negro mammy returned. I was now fifteen years of age, and more thoroughly imbued with the spirit of adventure than ever.

CHAPTER II.

NEW IDEALS—HUGH—THE KENTUCKIAN—OFF FOR
FORT GIBSON—MY FIRST RIFLE AND THE FIRST
INDIAN — MY FIRST NIGHT ON THE PLAINS —
ROUGHING IT—FIRST REQUEST FOR FOOD—FIRST
WILD GAME—MY HERO.

FROM this time on, I heard nothing more of my friend, The Healer. But if I had been disgusted with him, my first strange character, I was to be charmed with another whom I next met in the hotel office. This new acquaintance was a tall, raw-boned man, fully six feet, two inches in height, dressed entirely in buckskin and wearing a broad-brimmed hat and a long knife sticking in his belt. He was in every particular my ideal of the pictures I had seen, and of which I had read in the dime novels.

Being prompted by some impulse, I commenced a conversation with him, during which he told me he was "Kentuck Hugh" (a noted trapper and hunter), and that he had killed and scalped many wild Indians in his time. He remarked that he was leaving at once for Fort Gibson, in the Cherokee Territory, one hundred and twenty-five miles northwest from Fort Smith, and that he intended to walk the entire distance, sending his effects ahead by stage, with the exception of two blankets and a long rifle, of the old pattern, which he proposed to carry with him.

In suppressed excitement, I asked him if I might accompany him, and my joy knew no bounds when he replied in true backwoodsman style: "Sure! be glad to have you." On being appraised that I had no money, he paid my hotel bill, amounting to a dollar and twenty-five cents, and put his bundle and my carpet bag aboard the stage. We crossed the river in a flat-bottomed boat, and started on our way. How my whole being thrilled, and how my heart beat at the thought that I was going into a country of real live Indians. Heretofore I had never had a gun of any kind in my hand, and I longed to handle his, but dared not ask him that privilege.

We had walked but a short distance, when we saw a man coming on horseback. "Here comes an Indian." said Hugh, and my heart beat fast, expecting every moment to see Hugh kill and scalp him.

"How are you and where are you going?" the Indian asked, in very good English.

"To Fort Gibson," Hugh replied. "Are we on the right road?"

"Yes," was the Indian's reply. "This is the stage road and you can't go wrong."

He then asked Hugh if he had any whiskey with him, and said that if he would give him a drink, he would go back with us and give us dinner. My companion produced a small flask of Peach Brandy and gave the Indian a drink, whereupon he turned back with us. I was watching him very closely all the while, and thinking that he was a rather tame looking Indian, as he was dressed in white men's clothes. The only characteristics about him that to my mind were anything like those of an Indian, were his dark complexion and a few turkey feathers he wore in his hat.

After a short time we arrived at his house. Hugh took a drink from the flask and gave our Indian friend another drink; the latter then spoke to his squaw in the Cherokee tongue, ordering her to get our dinner. She complied, but not in the most gracious manner possible, looking daggers at us all the while.

Presently the dinner was ready, and a really good meal it was. The Indian retained the flask while we ate, and drank what was left. Before we had finished eating he came in, whooping and yelling in true Indian fashion and said to Hugh: "Don't you know that you can be arrested for bringing whiskey into the Indian Territory? Now if you don't give me some more, I'll have both of you arrested." Such is Indian gratitude.

I was badly frightened and expected every moment to see Hugh shoot him, but instead, Hugh was very mild and told the Indian he had no more with him. He even went so far as to open his shirt front and bundle of blankets, in order to convince the Indian he was telling the truth. I was disgusted with my companion. I supposed that Hugh, being an old Indian fighter, would surely kill this red-skin on the spot. Presently the Indian, seemingly satisfied that Hugh was not deceiving him, mounted his horse and went back down the road, yelling like mad.

We gathered up our blankets and started on our way, Hugh acting in a very sullen manner. After a little he said to me: "If it had not been for that Indian squaw, I would have killed him, dead sure." This raised Hugh a notch in my estimation, as I was beginning to think that he was not the ideal of my dime-novel education.

We trudged on until sundown, when we stopped for the night under a large oak tree. Hugh lighted the fire,—just as I had read in the novels,—spread out the blankets, and we laid down to sleep. This was my first night on the frontier. Sleep for me was impossible. When darkness came, a feeling of home-sickness came over me, and oh! how I wished myself back at home in my nice, clean bed. I fell to thinking of father, mother, sisters, brothers—ran the gamut of my friends and acquaintances in the old town and wondered what each was doing just then. I choked down many sobs that night, for I did not want Hugh to think I was not game.

At this time I was well dressed and was wearing low cut shoes, called Oxford ties. The heels were very high and were almost under the instep, and from that one day's walking in the hot sun and sand, my shoes were runover to one side and my feet very sore.

Morning came at last. The birds began to sing and Nature was awake again for another day. Hugh awoke, and after stretching himself and yawning a time or two, said: "Well, my boy! How do you feel?"

"Pretty good," I replied, "except that my feet are very sore."

He then took me to a spring close by and I bathed my feet, which helped greatly. We rolled up the blankets and ate some crackers and cold meat, which Hugh had brought along. It had never occurred to me how we were going to get any food, but I found out very soon. We trudged along until three o'clock in the afternoon, when we came to a house by the roadside. Hugh told me to go over and ask for something to eat, as neither of us had any money. I did not want to go and informed him that I had never begged in my life.

"You'll get used to that, my boy, before you're as old as I!" was his reply.

I summed up courage, choked down my pride, and knocked hard on the door, which was opened by a black squaw. I asked her for something to eat. She didn't seem to understand I was asking for food, so I began to make signs. These, too, were without avail; and so, neither of us being able to speak the other's tongue, the attempt was a failure and resulted in having the door shut in my face with a bang. I started back to Hugh, feeling very downcast at my unsuccessful appeal for food. On my way back, however, I noticed an old-fashioned cheese press with a cheese under it and a large stone on top for pressing. While watching the house closely to see if I was observed, I went to the press and stole the cheese,—my first theft. But I know, dear reader, you will forgive me this bit of wrong-doing; as one, when hungry, dead broke, and utterly unable to speak Cherokee, will do almost anything to secure something to eat.

Walking on about four miles, we came to a spring where we concluded to camp for the night. We ate the cheese and drank the spring water to wash it down, and, as a result, neither of us slept very much that night. Although a rather slim supper, the "quality" was there, and, consequently, we dreamed of everything imaginable during the little time we slept.

When morning came, we started on, and after a walk of an hour or so, arrived at a stage station kept by an old Irishman, with a heart as big as a barrel. He had just gotten up and greeted us with: "Top av the marnin to yez; ye air out early."

"Yes," my companion replied, "and very hungry at that." We were offered breakfast, which, however, had a string attached to it in the shape of a woodpile.

"Now, bhoys," said the Irishman, "here is a fine axe; chop me a bit of wood, and yez shall have a foine meal."

Hugh, being a fine axeman, we soon completed our task, Hugh doing the chopping and I carrying it in. Presently, breakfast was ready. The Irishman called us in and said: "Bhoys, ye're all right. Sit down and fill up; there's some venison."

I had not the remotest idea of what he meant by venison, and presently asked Hugh what it was.

"Deer meat, my boy," was his reply.

How delighted I was at the thought of eating my first wild game. Now I knew that all I had read in the dime novels was true. Before leaving, the Hibernian, noticing that I limped, gave me some coal oil with which to bathe my feet, and which helped them wonderfully. He also gave us food enough to last us two days, and told us we would find another stage station twenty-five miles farther on.

We started; I was satisfied with the world and everything in it. My feeling of home-sickness was entirely gone. About two o'clock in the afternoon we were still traveling when, on looking a short distance to one side of the road, I saw about a dozen turkeys.

"Hugh!" I exclaimed, "there are some turkeys; there must be a house near by."

"Hush!" he said, "those are wild turkeys." And before I could regain my senses, he dropped on one knee and fired. Down fell the largest bird, and unable to contain myself, I rushed after it and carried it back to Hugh in triumph.

"Pretty good shot. Turkey for supper tonight," said Hugh, as he reloaded his gun. One can imagine my admiration for him the remainder of the afternoon. I set him up for my hero, and to this day can see him walking ahead of me, I carrying the turkey. Hugh was a great walker, and kept me busy keeping up with him. I thought him the greatest man in the world, and that if some day I could be like him, the height of my ambition would be reached.

On arriving at the stage station, we ate the food furnished by our friend at the last station. After a good night's rest in the hayloft, we had turkey—roast turkey—for breakfast. We helped about the place, remaining all day that day to rest and finish up that turkey. We were well treated there, and I for one was loath to leave the place. Hugh entertained me all the while with accounts of his adventures with Indians and wild animals. How I admired that man! Why, I would have died for him any moment.

To me, our next day's journey was not so hard, as we were in the timber all day. We were protected from the rays of the sun and the sand was not as hot as it was at first. The woods were filled with wild doves, and to me their cooing was so sad that it made me homesick to hear them.

"Why don't you shoot some of them, Hugh?" I asked.

He looked at me in disgust. "Wait until we find some larger game, my boy," he replied. "We are almost out of the settlements and ought to get a shot at a deer soon." The thought of it thrilled me and I kept a good lookout, but saw no deer. We arrived at the third station about dark, but there the keeper was not so friendly as the others we had passed. After some talk, however, he thawed out and we found him to be a pretty good fellow. We trudged on again next day, stopping at another station that night. The following night we arrived at Fort Gibson.

CHAPTER III.

OUR WELL-TAGGED BAGGAGE—DESERTED—"TENDER-
FOOT"—A STRANGE OFFER OF MARRIAGE—THE
INDIAN ENGINEERING PARTY—AN OLD FRIEND—A
HORRIBLE PRACTICAL JOKE.

ON our arrival, we went to the hotel. Before entering, Hugh reminded me that he had no money, and advised me to say nothing about it while we were in the hotel. He boldly registered our names, and, as the stage office was in the hotel, he asked if our baggage had been left there by the stage.

"Yes," the clerk replied, producing it; mine, with a tag attached calling for four dollars, and Hugh's for three dollars.

The next morning Hugh informed me that he was going out on the grade to look for a job as bridge carpenter. The Missouri, Kansas & Texas Railroad was then grading its road about four miles west of Fort Gibson. Heretofore, I had supposed that the occupation of Indian fighters consisted entirely of hunting, trapping and slaying Indians, and was correspondingly disappointed in my hero on being told by him that he was going to work. We left the hotel early in the morning without settling our bills, and had walked about two miles, when we arrived at a spring, to the north of which was a wooded canyon. At this point Hugh left me, saying he was going into the brush to cut a couple of walking sticks, and requested that I wait where I was until he returned. After waiting about an hour, I began to think that some wild animal had eaten him. I was considerably frightened, and halooed to him. Receiving no response, I went up to the top of a near-by ridge, and from there saw the railroad graders at work. I ran to them in great

trepidation and told them that my partner was missing, and that I thought he had been eaten by wild
animals. They burst into a hearty laugh.

"Here is another tenderfoot," was their only reply.
The expression "tenderfoot," I had never heard before, and I naturally thought the graders referred to
my feet, which were very sore and tender and I felt
that had they walked as far as I, their feet would
have been in a like condition. Sometime afterward
I learned the term applied not to one's feet, but was
a common expression for a "greenhorn" in the
country.

I asked the graders for work, but was refused.
Then I returned to the hotel hoping to find or hear
something of Hugh, but was told they had not seen
him, so I came to the conclusion that he had deserted
me. I was homesick and heartbroken, and my ambition vanished—"great Indian fighters existed not in
reality, but on paper only."

I concluded that as I was alone I would go back
to Fort Smith, and asked the hotel man for my carpet
bag. He refused, however, to let me have it until I
paid him six dollars—two for the hotel and four for
the stage company; and no amount of pleading on
my part could soften his heart or change his decision.
Crestfallen, I departed from the hotel minus my
carpet bag; arriving at the first stage station that
night, footsore, weary, and discouraged. The station-
man took me in, giving me a good meal, and I enjoyed
a good night's rest. The next morning he offered to
engage me to dig potatoes for him, for which he
agreed to pay me fifty cents a day and my board and
lodging.

Here was the turning point in my career. I had
arrived at this station the previous evening with the
firm resolve to return to home and friends; the ardor

of western adventures had undergone a severe shock, and was at a decidedly low ebb. The ideals in which, in my boyish fancy, I had placed so much confidence, had completely vanished, and unpleasant memories alone remained with me for comfort and consolation. However, I felt induced to accept the offer of the station-man and for two weeks worked for him, digging potatoes.

During this time I had gradually gained courage and my adventurous spirit was again in the ascendancy. My efforts and diligence evidently met with favor in the eyes of my employer, for one day he called me into his room and asked me how I liked the country.

"Fairly well," I replied.

"Well," he rejoined, "do you want to become a rich man? If so, I will tell you how."

I looked at him without speaking, and he went on: "As you know, my wife is a Cherokee, and she has a sister just your age who has seen you and likes you. Her mother, who lives on the hill yonder, owns many head of cattle and horses, and a great deal of corn land, all under cultivation. She is old now, and when she dies the girl and my wife will get it all. There is a white man working for her mother who has been trying to marry the girl, but she prefers you and wants to meet you and will be here in the morning. I will do the talking for both, and can fix it up in a few minutes; then you can go to Fort Gibson and be married."

This man, Pat, was a big-hearted Irishman and meant well, but as for my getting married—well, I was not exactly in the mood for discussing matters of that nature just then.

True to the Irishman's word, the girl came the next day. She was astride a horse, bare back, and with only a rope loop in the horse's mouth for a bridle. She was a well-formed girl, but I could not fancy her for a wife, particularly for my wife. The Irishman talked to her in her native tongue (Cherokee) and then to me in English, but as I did not care to offend either of them, I told him I would think it over that night. He urged me to decide quickly before the other white man could secure the prize.

Later in the day a surveying party came into the station. It consisted of the chief and twenty-one men and two four-mule teams, and was engaged in running a railroad survey from Fort Smith, Arkansas, to connect with the main line of the Atlantic & Pacific Railway at Antelope Hills, three hundred miles south. After the party had camped in front of the station, the chief came in to obtain provisions, and they had a guide to take them through the Cherokee country, as it was difficult to find camping places. While in conversation with my Irish friend, the chief gave his name as Mr. Innes. My heart leaped into my mouth, for I remembered a Mr. Innes who was City Engineer in my home town. After he had made some purchases, I followed him out and asked him if he ever lived in Cape Vincent, New York.

"Born and raised there," was his reply.

"Then you must know my father, Captain Young?"

"Well, I should say I do," he ejaculated. "But what under the sun ever brought you into this country?"

"Don't know," I replied, ashamed to acknowledge that the little yellow covered novels were the cause of it. He took me over to his camp and talked to me for an hour, finally saying: "I can't let the son of an old schoolmate run wild out here. I don't really need any more help, but will put you on the pay roll at forty dollars per month, and your duties will be to carry the lunch bucket and give the transit man a back sight when he moves on ahead, and assist in making and numbering stakes when necessary."

Of course, this was all Greek to me, but I was to get away from that young squaw and had found my father's friend, and so was extremely happy. I related to my new friend the troubles I had been having about my carpet bag, and showed him my shoes; or rather, what was left of them, for they were almost gone. The next day he sent a man on horseback to Fort Gibson with six dollars to pay the charges on my carpet bag; and to my great joy, he returned with it.

We camped here for three days, and in the meantime Mr. Innes went over to a store on the north side of the river and purchased a pair of boots for me. They were about two sizes too large, but it was the best he could do. The old Irishman paid me what he owed me before we left. He was very much disappointed at the thought of losing a prospective brother-in-law, and I suppose that my would-be bride was almost heartbroken. I have seen neither of them since.

Many times since then I pondered over my extreme good fortune in unwittingly eluding the trap set for me by that wily Irish station-man. Shortly after our departure he erected a large building and entered into a co-operative plan with the Cherokees of that vicinity, which proved disastrous to them. The agreement entered into was to the effect that the Cherokees were each to contribute a certain number of Cherokee cattle, which the Irishman was to take to Kansas City, exchange same for staple products to be sold at the Co-Operative Store, and all share in the profits. They filled thirty cars with these cattle, and Pat took them to Kansas City, realized a fabulous sum and departed for parts unknown. Ever after his departure Pat was but a passing memory to his faithful Cherokee wife and all who knew him. This base deception made a lasting impression on the Cherokees, who up to this time had intermarried with the whites. For a long time afterward, they looked on every white man with supreme disgust and contempt.

We left there under the guidance of an Indian, furnished us by the old Irishman. This guide made himself generally useful, in more ways than one. He was thoroughly familiar with the various waterholes, and without him we would certainly have fared badly.

Being a tenderfoot, I was the butt of all the jokes played in the camp by those twenty-one men, and Mr. Innes was as bad as any of them. On my second day with the outfit they played a horrible practical joke on me. That is, it was horrible as far as I was concerned.

The four-mule teams were in charge of a character who was known by the name of "California Jack." This man was noted as a practical joker and was particularly fond of telling stories of early life in California in which he had centered as the principal figure.

At night we slept side by side in a large tent, using our blankets for bedding, and with our feet toward the entrance. Before we went to sleep that night, "California Jack" told a most dreadful snake story. He said that once, while in California, he and two others were asleep in a tent, just as we were, when a rattle-snake crawled under one of the boy's blankets and coiled himself up on the boy's breast, and he knew that if he moved, the snake would bite him, which meant certain death, and that the only way to save his life was to keep perfectly still until the snake had its sleep out. According to the teamster's story, the snake crawled away after a while, but the boy's scare was so great that he died of fright within ten minutes after the snake left his breast, and was buried the next day. "And it is a strange fact," added Jack, "that snakes seem to know boys. Many times in California I have known them to attack boys and yet never bother men."

"Oh, let us go to sleep," interrupted the other men. "We have to get up early."

In a few minutes all of them were apparently sound asleep, when I felt something slimy touch my bare leg. Up it crawled to my breast. I thought of Jack's warning and kept still, but oh, how frightened I was. I thought I would die. Presently, I could stand it no longer, and jumped clear over the two men who were sleeping on my left. Everyone sprang up and wanted to know what the matter was. "Snakes!" was all I could say.

"Oh, you are dreaming," they replied.

"No," I persisted, "I saw him, and he was ten feet long."

"Yes," added Jack, "they grow that long in this country." We then shook all the blankets, but finding nothing, concluded that the snake had escaped through one of the openings.

We all laid down again, but there was no more sleep for me. I was on the lookout for snakes. In a few minutes everyone was snoring once more, when again I felt that slimy snake crawling up my bare leg. I stood it as long as I could, then grabbed for it and, as I supposed, caught it by the head.

"Wake up, boys!" I yelled. "I have him!" Everyone jumped up—Jack telling me to hold the snake fast while he lighted a candle. I looked at the supposed snake and discovered that it was only a cattail; a kind of weed or rush that grows in swamps. Jack had dampened the head or top of it, and it was he who was doing the trick. All laughed, and that ended the fun.

It is a fact, however, that it was a bad country for snakes. There was also a large cricket in that part of the country, which made a noise exactly like a rattlesnake and which startled me very often, to the great amusement of the boys. The transition from "tenderfoot" to the state of stolidity, which gradually relieved me from the position of being the butt of others' jokes, though gradual, was in due time accomplished.

CHAPTER IV.

IN THE CREEK INDIAN COUNTRY—THE SEMINOLES—
THE SAC AND FOX INDIANS—ONCE MORE A VICTIM
—CARRIED OFF BY A NAKED INDIAN—THE SHAW-
NESS—ATLANTIC & PACIFIC RAILWAY SURVEY—
"BILL HENDERSON," THE HALF-BREED — FIRST
CATTLE HERDING—LOST ON THE RANGE.

WE worked in this vicinity for a while, and later went into the Creek Indian country. The Creeks, like the Cherokees, were civilized, and had good houses and schools. We next struck the Seminoles. These Indians were crossed to a great extent with the Negroes, as before the war a great many Creeks and Seminoles owned slaves. They intermarried with the squaws, producing very dark offspring. We encountered the Sac and Fox Indians on our next move. This tribe was at that time blanket Indians and of fine physique, many of them being six feet in height. A few of them exceeding even this mark. They lived in lodges made of the skins of elks and other animals, and had their faces painted in various colors. Many of them are now immensely wealthy, through the recent discovery of oil on their land. This was my first sight of real blanket Indians, and I found, much to my surprise, that they were not warlike at all, but were frightful beggars. It was here again that I began to think that dime novels had not told me the truth. We changed guides at each Indian tribe, as each guide went with us through his own country only.

I dared not tell any of the boys that I had run away from home for the purpose of fighting Indians, for fear that they would laugh at me. I, however, grew wiser from day to day, and, as I attained

further wisdom, it became more and more difficult
for them to play tricks upon me. Although I had
been progressing in this line, the boys assisted by
the Indian guide, did play another trick upon me,
while in the Sac and Fox country.

Just before we left the line in the evening to go
into camp, Mr. Innes asked me to go back about a
mile and look at a certain stake. To do this, I had
to go across a low place, out of sight of the other
boys. To my surprise, I was stopped by an Indian,
who was painted and almost naked. He rushed at
me, caught me by the arm, and with his foot lifted
me up before him on his pony, and yelling as only
an Indian can yell, rapidly rode off with me. I wanted
to yell myself, but was too frightened to do so. However, this was scarcely necessary, for the Indian made
enough of that kind of noise to answer for both. I
fought hard to escape from him, but all to no purpose.
The reader can imagine my feelings, as I had every
reason to believe that I had been made a captive by
the savage. Dime novels had told the truth, after all.

We rode for some time, and presently came in
sight of the camp. There were the boys, waving
their hats and laughing. It was the guide, disguised,
who had played the trick on me; to say I was relieved, would be putting it mildly.

We next entered the domain of the Shawness, but
they would not permit us to pass through their
country. Mr. Innes met them at a council held under
a large clump of oak trees, at which all the Indians
wore their blankets, and were painted in their war
colors. To me it was a great sight. Mr. Innes,
through an interpreter furnished by their agent, informed them that he and his party were only looking
through the country by request of the Great Father
in Washington.

"No," they replied. "You can go no farther; you are bad men and must go back." Mr. Innes then attempted to bluff them, by telling them he would send for the soldiers, but all to no avail. And after a three days' council, we started back to the nearest town—Prairie City, the then terminus of the Atlantic & Pacific Railroad. We had been out for four months, and on our return, were paid off, and the party disbanded. I heard later that Mr. Innes continued the work the following year, under escort of cavalry.

In company with Frank Emmons, one of the party, we walked to Fort Gibson, where I again inquired for my friend Hugh, but found no one who knew anything of him.

The following day we left Fort Gibson and walked to Chetopa, Kansas—the then terminus of the Missouri, Kansas & Texas Railway. Here that road entered the Cherokee Territory. After spending our money, we went south six miles in search of work. Later, we were employed to pitch hay for "Bill" Henderson, a half breed Cherokee, and a veritable devil when he was under the influence of liquor. A company of St. Louis people had leased his wild hay land, paying him so much per acre for the privilege of cutting the hay, which, after cutting, was stacked, baled and shipped to St. Louis. I became quite expert in the work, but later on had some trouble with the boss and quit. I was indeed fortunate, being the only one who received pay for labor done, as the company became insolvent and none of the others received a cent of wages. There was no recourse, as the hay was in the Indian Territory and could not be held for amounts due. On severing my connection with Henderson, I returned to Chetopa. There I met a Mr. Pancake, who owned some eight hundred head of cattle, which he had driven from Texas, and who hired me as a herder. Of course, in this work it was necessary for me to ride a horse, which was a new experience. The horse and saddle supplied me, I looked on with some misgivings, as I dared not tell Mr. Pancake that I had never ridden a horse, and waited until he was out of sight before attempting to mount. Although it was but twenty miles to the herd, I believe I rode twice that distance before reaching there. I made the resolve that if I wanted to hold that job, I must learn to ride, and I did, but how sore I was the next morning!

I shall never forget the first night I was sent out on guard. In those days we stood two hours' watch in the night, riding around the cattle while they were "bedded" down, and singing to them most of the time. My saddle horse was not a cow pony, but an Indian pony which Mr. Pancake had purchased in the Indian Territory. After I had ridden around the cattle for a while, I began to doze. Presently I looked to my right, but could not see the cattle. The night was dark, and my pony had strayed away. Had he been a cow pony, he would have stayed with the herd, as they are used to cattle. I tried to find them, but being unsuccessful, began to shout, hoping that the boys in camp would hear me. I rode for some time, and finally concluded that I was lost. I stopped my tired pony and hobbled him with the bridle rein, as I had no lariat. Using the saddle for a pillow, and covering myself with the saddle blanket, I attempted to sleep, but without success. What troubled me most was, the thought that I had the boss' gold watch, which he loaned to each herder that he might know the time to call the relief. I was sure they would miss me and think that I had run away with the pony and watch. I found out later that my surmise was correct.

When daylight came, I saw a campfire in the distance. Riding over, I found a negro cook preparing the morning meal and told him that I was looking for Pancake's herd, but did not tell him I was lost. "Well," he replied, "you are a long way from it. They are camped on Pond Creek, eight miles southeast of here." After taking breakfast with him, I started for the herd, and arrived there in due time. Four of the boys were out looking for me, supposing that I had run away with the watch and pony. When I explained the situation to the boss, he blamed the Indian pony for all the trouble. This relieved me very much.

These cattle had just arrived from Texas over the Chisholm trail and were being kept here to rest and fatten, after which they were to be sold and shipped east by rail. A period of three months was usually required to make the drive from Texas.

I had been with Mr. Pancake about a month, when a man named Hamilton, from Arkansas City, Kansas, bought two hundred head of stock cattle out of the herd, and employed a Mr. Sutherland to help care for them. Mr. Sutherland and his wife camped near. They were from Texas and were looking for Government land, and had a wagon and four head of horses.

Mr. Sutherland engaged me to go with him. Hamilton, who later proved to be a perfect devil, bought a pair of gentle oxen and hitched them to the wagon. We rode the horses and drove the cattle. We had not been out many days, when the two men quarreled and had it not been for Mrs. Sutherland, Hamilton would surely have been killed, as Sutherland, having a violent temper, had already killed two men in Texas some time previously. For that reason he had been compelled to leave there. Three nights after the trouble between Hamilton and Sutherland, two horse thieves traveling through the country, plying their vocation, stole our horses and we had no alternative but to follow them on foot. Sutherland having spent his entire life on the frontier of Texas, was a wonderful trailer, and by signs and foot prints, with which he was thoroughly accustomed, accomplished what to me seemed an utter impossibility. Taking with us sufficient food to provide against hunger, we walked for three days, at the end of which time we discovered our horses in an open cornfield. Sutherland ordered me to keep quiet, suggesting I lie down in the grass and rest. I asked him, "Why not go and get the horses?" He replied: "Do as I tell you. I will attend to the horses." This I did, and was soon curled up in the grass fast asleep. Suddenly I was awakened by two rapid gun shots, and I jumped up and ran over to Sutherland, who said to me: "Remain here, and I will go over and get the horses; those horse thieves will never bother any one again." Sutherland left me and shortly returned with the horses, two six-shooters, a Henry rifle (the first I had ever seen), and considerable ammunition. He presented me with one of the six-shooters. I was naturally proud of this six-shooter, as I had never had one of my own, and used it until the cartridge pistol came into use. We then returned to the camp, where we were welcomed by Hamilton and Mrs. Sutherland, who were nearly worn out by herding the cattle on foot in our absence. Seeing the extra gun and six-shooters, Hamilton asked Sutherland where he got them. Sutherland replied in a very cool and unconcerned manner: "Oh, I borrowed them from a couple of friends of mine."

From that time, I never knew Sutherland to mention the matter again, but am satisfied that he killed both horse thieves.

You must bear in mind, dear reader, that these events transpired in 1866, at which time wrongs and grievances, fancied and real, were avenged not by a court of justice, but by the principals, in their rough, stern way. This was the only known and recognized law in that country at that time and for years to come.

After many hardships, we arrived at Hamilton's ranch, near Arkansas City. Here we received our wages, and after another quarrel with Hamilton, we went south, to what was then known as the Cherokee Strip.

CHAPTER V.

THE CHEROKEE STRIP—A SQUATTER—OUSTED BY
UNCLE SAM—UNWELCOME VISITORS—THE BANK
ROBBERS—MY HAIR TRIGGER RIFLE—WITH THE
OSAGE INDIANS—BUCKETS OF REAL SNAKES—BIG
FIGHT BETWEEN LONG AND SHORT HORNS, AT
NEWTON, KANSAS.

I WILL here present to you items of interest pertaining to the Cherokee Strip, including many stirring incidents which have from time to time been a matter of public record. The Strip was a piece of land owned by the Cherokee Indians, about one hundred miles square. It adjoined Howard County, Kansas, five miles south of the town of Elgin. I afterward heard that Howard County had been subdivided by the Government, and a portion of it called Elk County.

A report gained currency that the United States Government intended buying this strip and allowing 160 acres to each person having homestead or squatter rights. Sutherland and I concluded to make a location, and accordingly, settled ourselves on adjoining pieces of land, but lived together. In the meantime, the Osage Indians sold their lands in Kansas and bought this strip from the Cherokees, before the Government had concluded the deal. When they came to take possession of it, they discovered that it had been taken up by the white people. The houses which we had built were of logs cut off the ridges, where post oak grew plentifully. The houses were without floors. The cooking was done in old-fashioned fireplaces. The houses were few and far between; this being particularly true of the section where we lived.

One clear, moonlight night we were suddenly awakened by a loud rapping. I opened the door, while Mr.

Sutherland stood just to one side with his Spencer carbine ready for instant use. There I found three mounted men, all armed to the teeth, and the hardest looking trio I ever saw. After asking who lived there, they wanted to know if I were alone.

"No," I answered, "Mr. Sutherland and wife are here." Whereupon Sutherland stepped out from his hiding place.

We were instructed by the unwelcome visitors that they wanted something to eat at once. I was ordered to take their horses to the corral and feed them, which I did. Although it was nearly midnight, they compelled Mrs. Sutherland to get up and prepare them something to eat. One of their number, with gun in hand, remained on guard on the outside and after the other two had eaten, he came in and partook of the food. When all had eaten, they went to the corral where they spent the remainder of the night sleeping, each taking turns at guard duty. At daylight they came back to the house and the spokesman asked us if we had any money. We told him "No," as we had not yet raised a crop.

"Well," he said, handing me three twenty-dollar greenbacks, "we will stake you. Give the man and the woman one each and keep the other for yourself."

They then asked: "Does anyone live in that house yonder?" pointing to a house about two miles distant.

"Yes," I replied; "Mr. Kruger lives there."

"Has he any horses?"

"Yes, four head."

Whereupon they saddled up and left, we noticing that their horses had a tired and jaded appearance. In about two hours, Kruger came to our house with his head bandaged up, and said that one of the men had struck him with a six-shooter. Kruger was a contrary German, and, having served in the army, thought that he was king of the earth. He probably became saucy when they wanted to trade horses with him. They accordingly clubbed him, took three of his best animals, and left their own in place of them. Had he used better judgment under the conditions, he might have made a good trade with them. He wanted us to go with him and try to recover his horses, and became very angry when we refused to do so.

Three days later a sheriff with three deputies, in pursuit of these men, arrived at our cabin and made inquiries concerning them. We informed them that three men had stopped over night with us and had gone on, heading west. They then proceeded on their way but returned the following day, having evidently given up the chase, and informed us that the men they were hunting were outlaws who robbed a bank in Parsons, Kansas, killing two men who had attempted to arrest them. The sheriff and his deputies remained with us over night, departing early in the morning. We were careful not to tell them that the outlaws had given us any money. The next day Sutherland and I went to town and bought many necessaries in the way of clothing, groceries, etc. The storekeeper expressed considerable surprise when we handed him our greenbacks, as this form of money in that country was very scarce in those days.

One bright morning not long after these events, Sutherland and I went together on a deer hunt; he took his Spencer carbine, and I borrowed a heavy muzzle-loading rifle, equipped with a set trigger. I was now to have my first experience at deer hunting.

Sutherland proceeded with caution along the top of a ridge or hill, and I along the foot. I had not gone far when I saw three deer pawing in the snow, looking for acorns. They had not seen me, and I quickly decided that here was the chance to secure my first deer. Unfortunately, while in the act of taking aim, I unconsciously touched the set-trigger, resulting in the load going off in the ground about ten feet from me. Hearing the shot, Mr. Sutherland ran down and asked me if I had hit a deer. Not wanting him to know that my rifle had been discharged accidentally, I replied: "Yes, I hit him." Whereupon he began to search, but no deer could be found. Mr. Sutherland scolded me severely for my poor marksmanship, and we returned home without any game.

In the meantime, the Osages promptly appealed to the government, and the latter notified us to vacate. We refused, as we had improved the land to a large extent by building rail fences, log houses, etc. The government then sent troops and six-mule teams there and moved us across the line into Kansas, giving the Osages peaceful possession. This was, of course, just, although we did not consider it so at the time.

In the spring of 1867 the Osage Indians established their new agency forty miles south of the Kansas line. The location selected was at the base of a rocky hill, which was infested with thousands of snakes. While digging a well, it was our custom every morning to lower a man in a bucket to the bottom. This was for the purpose of killing snakes that had fallen into the opening during the night.

There were twenty white men employed on this agency, and the agent had selected an Indian by the name of "Red Feather," who was to keep us supplied with deer meat. One day, the agency's interpreter, who was a white man, asked Red Feather how it happened that he always had a full supply of venison. Red Feather replied: "Some time I catch um deer and some time dog; white man don't know." For a time the interpeter kept this information to himself, but finally, it being too rich to keep, told us. Our feelings can be better imagined than described. Suffice to say that Red Feather had his contract cancelled on very short notice, and our fondness for deer meat vanished. For a long time afterward, we could not bear the mention of it.

Finally, becoming tired of agency life, and my roving disposition as I thought requiring a change, I started for the new town of Wichita, Kansas, which at that time was a shipping point for Texas cattle. I remained there but a short time. From Wichita I went to Newton, Kansas—then the terminus of the Atchison, Topeka & Santa Fe Railroad, and one of the wildest towns in the state. Newton was a rendezvous for gamblers and "sure-thing" men. There were numerous saloons and two large dance halls, a few merchandise stores and a hotel. At this particular time, the female element consisted entirely of dance-hall girls. The majority of the male population were, what were then termed, gun-fighters; the six-shooter being the only recognized law there at that time.

Here I witnessed one of the most noted gun fights that ever took place in the West. The fight was between Kansas and Texas desperadoes. It occurred in Tim Shea's dance-hall, and was a pre-arranged affair. The Texicans had visited the town some five days prior to this and ran things to suit themselves. They then sent word that they were coming back on a certain night and proposed to duplicate the act. Tim Shea gathered together about thirty Kansas gun-men whom he knew and could depend upon. True to their threat, the Texicans arrived on the appointed night. Shea, hearing them coming, stationed his men at the rear of the dance-hall; the Texicans riding up to the front, entered the door, yelling and shooting off their guns. Shea's men rushed in the back door, and the shooting began. The lights were shot out, all was darkness, and the entire thing was over in fifteen minutes. When the lamps were relighted, fourteen were found lying dead on the floor, but the number of wounded will never be known. One of the dance-hall girls was wounded in the right eye, and ever afterward was known as "One-eyed Molly." Few, if any, who took part in that fight are alive today. I will give you the names of a few of the prominent ones: Matt Reilly, Billy Brooks, Tim Shea, Lushey Bill, Chris Gilson, Tom Sherman, Pony Spencer. There were others whose names I cannot recall.

From Newton, I followed the extension of the Atchison, Topeka & Santa Fe Railroad to the next terminus, which was Larnerd, Kansas.

CHAPTER VI.

THE SANTE FE'S EXTENSION WEST—THE KANSAS PA-
CIFIC MAN-KILLING CELEBRETIES—"WILD BILL" OF
HAYES CITY—GREEN RIVER SMITH—PHIL COLE'S
FRUITLESS TACTICS—KANSAS BUFFALO—THE BUF-
FALO EXTERMINATED IN TWO YEARS.

THERE was probably no railroad extension westward ever marked by more lawlessness than was that of the Atchison, Topeka & Santa Fe. The next terminus was Dodge City, two miles west of Fort Dodge, and of which I will speak later.

Leaving Larnerd, I concluded to go northward to Hayes City, which at that time was the terminus of the Kansas Pacific Railroad, now a part of the Union Pacific system. It was there that I first met J. B. Hickok, better known as "Wild Bill." Bill was marshal of Hays City.

A good many stories have been written from time to time of this character, Wild Bill, but I am sure none will prove of more interest to the reader than that which I am about to relate. From the time of our first meeting in Hayes City, my remarks are based on personal knowledge and contact with him, dating from the year 1868 when we first met, to the time of his death, which occurred in 1876.

Our first meeting is indelibly impressed upon my mind. I had been dancing all night in one of the numerous dance-halls of Hayes City, as was the almost universal custom in those days of strangers looking for pleasure and entertainment. Morning found me waiting outside for one of the dance-hall girls, for whom I had formed a boyish fancy. The night's entertainment had proved costly to me, my

finances having dwindled from forty dollars to a
dollar and a half. This extravagance on my part
had been noted by Wild Bill, unknown to me. As I
stood on the sidewalk, deliberating, someone touched
me on the shoulder. I turned, and found myself
face to face with the finest looking man I have ever
seen or ever expect to see; a man who excited my
greatest admiration. He was about six feet, two
inches in height; perfectly formed and of strong
physique, and at that time thirty-one years old. He
had long auburn hair, and clear blue eyes; eyes that
showed kindness and friendship to all, except the evil
doer, to whom they meant the reverse. I was naturally
drawn toward him, and instinctively felt that no
matter how tough the town or its lawless characters,
I had met a friend. He asked me where I hailed from
and I replied: "From the Santa Fe Construction." He
gave me some very wholesome advice regarding spending my money so foolishly and asked me what I was
doing at Hayes City. I told him I was looking for
work. After a long pause, during which he appeared
to be sizing me up, he asked me if I could drive a
six-mule team. I could not, and frankly told him so.
He evidently thought I could learn quickly, for he
took me into a near-by saloon and taught me how to
tie a Government hame-string. The Government at
that time used a leather strap with a knot on the end
of it instead of the buckle and tongue of the present
day.

The next morning he went with me to Fort Hayes,
two and a half miles distant. There we met the
corral boss, and Wild Bill asked him to put me to
work, stating that he had taken a fatherly interest in
me and wanted to see me get along in good shape. The
corral boss asked if I could drive a six-mule team. To
which Bill replied: "Yes." A mule collar was thrown
on the ground and I was told to tie the hames on,
which I did. He then turned to Bill with a broad

grin and remarked, "You have drilled him well." He then told me to remain at the post and he would put me to work. During the day I got acquainted with some of the mule drivers, who showed me how to harness a six-mule team. The term used for mule drivers in those days was "mule-skinners." The second morning Bill came out to see how I was getting along, and to his astonishment found me driving a six-mule team. He rode by my side for some distance, giving me pointers that afterward were very useful to me. I worked at this post for six months, during which I saw a great deal of Wild Bill, as I was in town nearly every night.

I will now give you this wonderful character's life as told to me by Bill himself, at my request three months previous to his death in Deadwood.

Wild Bill was born in Homer, Illinois, in 1837. His proper name was James Benson Hickok. He enlisted in the Union Army in 1862, and became a spy, operating principally in Missouri at the time when General Price of the Confederate Army was terrorizing the country with his lawless and merciless deeds. Bill's duties as a spy necessitated his connecting himself with General Price's command. As a result, he rendered invaluable services to the Union. He was discharged in 1865. He then went to Springfield, Missouri, at which place he killed his first man in civil life,—a character by the name of Dave Tutt, who had served in the Confederate Army and who had a great reputation as a gun-fighter. The circumstances of this killing, which occurred on July 28th, 1865, (and were verified by me on the county records of Springfield), were as follows:

On the night previous to July 28th, 1865, Tutt and Bill were engaged in a game of cards, in which Bill lost all of his ready cash. This resulted in his borrowing twenty dollars from Tutt and handing him his

watch as security, the loan to be repaid the following
morning. Bill was on hand at the appointed time,
but when he made a tender of the twenty dollars, Dave
refused to return the watch, claiming that the
amount borrowed was forty dollars instead of twenty.
Bill's indignation was further increased by Dave's
tantalizing remark that at twelve o'clock he would
walk across the public square with Bill's watch in his
pocket. Bill's reply to this insult was: "Sometimes
dead men wear watches!" Thus the matter ended
for the time being. Promptly at the stroke of twelve
o'clock Dave stepped out of the court house, Bill
approaching from an opposite direction. As they
spied each other, their hands went instinctively to
their guns, both quickly realizing that a life must
pay the forfeit. Bill's aim was steady and true, a
bullet through Dave's heart being the result, while
Dave's bullet went harmlessly over Bill's head. Thus
had Bill's prophecy come true.

Shortly after this occurrence, Bill left Springfield
and went to St. Louis, Missouri, where he was employed by Ben Holladay, who at that time was operating the Overland Stage Line from St. Louis to
San Francisco. Holladay had suffered no end of trouble
from gangs of desperadoes who were continually
holding up his stage coaches, robbing the passengers
and making off with the Wells Fargo strong box,
which was carried under contract.

Foremost among these desperadoes and the most
feared was the noted McCanless gang. Bill was given
instructions to exterminate this gang, which consisted
of nine men. He was asked how many men he would
require to assist him and replied: "None!" This was
certainly a good evidence of the man's grit and pluck.
Leaving St. Louis single handed, he made his initial
move by going to Rock Springs station on the Cim-
aron river, arriving at about four o'clock in the

afternoon and assuming charge immediately. He had been in his new quarters but one hour when McCanless, the leader of the gang, rode up and asked him what he was doing there. Bill replied that he was the "new station agent." McCanless' response was, that if he (Bill) was not away from there within twenty-four hours, he would be shipped to St. Louis in a box. Bill's reply was that when they returned, they would still find him on the job, for he had come to stay. True to McCanless' word, the gang did return on the following afternoon and gave bill the hardest battle of his life. Approaching the station, in which Bill was quartered, they opened fire on him,—nine men against one. They certainly were hardly prepared for what was to follow.

In less time than it takes to write this, Bill had shot four of them; but at this critical moment, his gun was knocked from his hand. Seizing a knife from the belt of McCanless, Bill used it to advantage. Again good fortune seemed to favor him, for regaining his gun, he speedily exterminated the remainder of the gang, except one, who had gotten some distance away. One more shot from Bill's six-shooter, and the extermination of the gang was complete.

Bill had not escaped unharmed. When he was found by a stocktender shortly after the battle, he was lying on his side unconscious and not a charge left in his gun. He had received three bullet and two knife wounds, which wounds came very nearly ending his useful career. He was taken immediately to St. Louis, where his life hung by a thread for a long time, but his remarkable vitality finally predominated. It was, however, fully a year before he was restored to his full mind and vigor.

In the fall of 1867, Bill's restless, roving disposition again began to assert itself. He left St. Louis; this time going to Camp Supply and Fort Sill in the

Indian Territory, not far south of Fort Dodge, Kansas.
At Camp Supply, he was engaged by the Government
as a scout. This vocation he followed for about a
year, which was brought to a close by his meeting
General Custer, of Indian fame. Custer was en route
to Fort Hayes and prevailed on Bill to go with him.
While scouting out of Fort Hayes, the town of Hayes
City sprung up. This town, like all other terminus
towns of early days, had its full quota of the lawless element and the question of keeping them in sub-
jection was a hard problem to solve. This particular
town got so bad that General Custer was appealed to
for military assistance, which he refused. He told
the citizens that he had a scout working for him by
the name of Wild Bill, and that if they could arrange
with him, he would guarantee that the lawless element
would be kept under control. These arrangements
were finally made and Wild Bill became the first
marshal of Hayes City. This was in the year 1868.
A marshal of those days was very different from what
the reader today might naturally suppose. He was
employed by the better class to maintain peace and
order, and his word and acts were the recognized law;
there being no court of justice in existence at that
time, neither had a marshal any power invested in
him by the Government.

Bill was a man of great characteristics, of magnetic
power, and probably the quickest man with a six-
shooter the world has ever produced. He was never
known to shoot twice at the same man, the first shot
in every case meaning certain death. (This brings my
story of Wild Bill down to the time when we first
met).

While Bill was marshal of Hayes City, I witnessed
his killing of seven soldiers, the circumstances of
which were as follows:

There were fifteen soldiers in the party, one of them being a 1st Sergant, with whom Bill had previously had trouble at Fort Hayes. This had resulted in ill feeling between the two, and further trouble was certain. Meeting Bill on the street at Hayes City, the sergeant having imbibed very freely and throwing caution to the winds, invited Bill to put away his guns and engage with him in a bare fist fight. To this Bill readily consented and, handing his guns to his friend, Paddy Walch, a saloon keeper, Bill and the sergeant went into the street to fight it out. Bill knocked the sergeant down three times. The soldiers, seeing their sergeant getting the worst of it, rushed in on Bill, one from behind placing his knee in the small of Bill's back, forcing him to the ground, the others in front kicking and striking at him. At this juncture Walch, fearing that Bill would be killed, came running up, handed Bill his guns and told him to use them if he valued his life. Without one instant's hesitation Bill seized his guns and commenced a rapid fire, killing two soldiers back of him by shooting over his right shoulder, at the same time killing five more in front with the gun in his left hand. Naturally this created great excitement, as killing a soldier, even by a town marshal, was a very serious affair those days. Bill, knowing that General Custer would give the matter a very thorough investigation, decided to leave the town and secrete himself in the hills until this was over.

General Custer decided that Bill was justified in the killing and exonerated him from all blame. Bill then resumed his duties as marshal. In the discharge of his duties while marshal of that town, he had a record of killing twelve men.

In the spring of 1869, the town of Abilene, Kansas, sprang up. This town was composed of an entirely different element from Hayes City, but the toughness predominated to a still larger extent, if such a thing were possible. Abilene was the rendezvous of cattlemen and cowboys, who drove large herds of cattle from Texas to Abilene, from where they were shipped to eastern markets. Naturally, Abilene became the scene of the wildest disorder; being marked by drunken orgies, carousals without number, and numerous shooting scrapes that were the natural result.

The first marshal of Abilene was one Green River Smith. This man, fearless and endowed with plenty of nerve, and having a very good opinion of himself, made many boasts; one of which was, that a bullet had never been moulded that could kill him. A short time after this boast, he was doomed to death, but in a different way from that of a bullet.

Taking his deputy with him, he left Abilene in search of two horse thieves who had been very troublesome to many. The thieves were located in a dug-out, three miles from town. Smith stationed his deputy at the entrance, he himself going inside. While in there, his deputy for some unexplained cause became alarmed and disappeared. One of the horse thieves, stepping behind Smith, struck him in the head with an axe, killing him and decapitated him. The news of Smith's death at the hands of the horse thief quickly reached Abilene, and for two months afterward the town was completely in the hands of the lawless element; in fact, the state of affairs had reached such a stage that the law-abiding citizens were seriously contemplating abandoning the town. At this critical time, a man who had just arrived from Hayes City remarked that if they could but secure Wild Bill, their troubles would be over. This was met with instant favor and resulted in Wild Bill becoming their next marshal.

Now, dear readers, we will pause for a moment as I wish to impress more vividly on your mind the

state of affairs as they existed at this time, also the
Herculean task Wild Bill had before him. Here was
a town that for two months had been in the hands of
a drunken, desperate, frenzied mob. Many men even
of that day would have hesitated had they been
placed in the position of Wild Bill and allotted
the necessary work he was to set out to do, in
order to completely change the conditions of the town.
I went to Abilene about four weeks before Bill and
remember distinctly the day he arrived there. It was
about four o'clock in the afternoon. He received a
warm welcome from the law-abiding citizens. The
news of his coming had preceded him, and was treated
by the lawless element as a huge joke. They had had
things their own way for so long without opposition,
that the idea of a single man subduing them was, from
their point of view, simply ridiculous. Bill commenced
business immediately upon his arrival. His first order
was that all men should disarm. Entering one of
the largest saloons, called "The Bullshead," Bill encountered a number of cow-punchers and ordered them
to disarm. This order was met with jeers and deris-
ion; some reaching defiantly for their guns. Bill, ever
on the alert, whipped out his guns and his rapid fire
quickly snuffed out the lives of eight men. This
action had a magic effect, and the manager of the
saloon (Ed Norton) was for a time kept busy receiving the guns handed him by those who had suddenly
decided that discretion was the better part of valor.
This was Bill's first official act in Abilene; temporarily,
it had a depressing effect. For a short time they
seemed to feel that they had more than met their
master. As this feeling gradually wore off, a number
of them collected in a dance-hall where they concocted
a plan to assassinate him. This was, fortunately,
overheard by a man named Billy Mullen, who had
known Bill in Hayes City. Mullen quickly made his
way to The Bullshead saloon and appraised Bill of

the plot. Bill went immediately to the dance-hall and ordered all who were in there to back up against the wall and put their six-shooters on the floor at their feet. Meeting, as he has expected, with some opposition, and being a man who took no chances, Bill immediately began shooting, killing five before it was fully realized that he was indeed their master.

I will narrate one more episode that occurred in this town. There was a certain character who went by the name of "Shang,"—so named from his great height. Shang was a wealthy Texas cattle man. He employed about two hundred cow-punchers or cowboys, as they are called now-a-days, and large droves of his cattle were constantly being driven in to Abilene. Shang's power among this certain class, owing to his immense wealth, was supreme. It was not unusual for him to have an enemy killed for a money consideration. Shang and Bill had fallen out, as the result of a fancied grievance, and Shang decided that Bill's life should pay the forfeit.

For this purpose he sent to Texas for a man named Phil Cole, a noted Texas gun-fighter with a reputation in that state, equal to Bill's in Kansas. The agreement was that Cole was to come to Abilene and kill Bill, for which Shang was to pay him one thousand dollars. On Cole's arrival Shang met him on the outskirts of the town, taking him down to the corral and taking the precaution to have Cole remove his six-shooters and spurs, so as not to arouse any suspicion. I do not believe at that particular time that Bill thought for a moment that Shang had sent for Cole. Bill and Cole had never seen each other, and they knew each other by reputation only. Shang's desire was to point out Bill to Cole without arousing Bill's suspicions. Shang and Cole left the corral together, going to The Bullshead saloon, where he pointed out Bill to Cole. Cole, when he looked this great man over, and having heard so much of him through Shang, completely lost his nerve. But knowing what he was brought there for and also knowing that he must make good to Shang, Cole asked Shang to walk back down to the corral with him; where together they talked the matter over. Shang finally went home. Cole, after Shang had left him, conceived the idea of taking a dog that was in the corral, tying a rope around its neck, arming himself, and later taking the dog to The Bullshead. This decided upon, he started off with the dog at about half past one o'clock in the morning. On reaching the saloon, he tied the dog to the door latch, and stood behind an awning post in front of the door. Knowing that Bill was on the inside, he shot the dog, expecting Bill to run out in the dark to see what the shooting was about. Bill was not to be caught in this trap. Instead of running out, with gun in hand he opened the door, keeping behind it until the light shone from the saloon into the street, when he saw Cole peeking from behind the awning post. They both shot at the same time; Bill a fraction of a second quicker than Cole and his bullet entering Cole's heart, killed him instantly. Thus ended the career of the greatest gun-fighter Texas ever produced.

While Marshal of Abilene, Bill was compelled to kill twenty-five men, but he had been successful in his mission and had transformed Abilene into a peaceful, law-abiding towr

In the following year, 1870, the cattle business began to spread out and new towns were springing up, and vieing with Abilene as a cattle center. Among these was the town of Ellsworth, which was sorely in need of a fearless marshal. Bill transferred his base of operations to that town, but did not meet with the opposition he had met with in Abilene. By this time, his reputation had spread far and wide and the majority of the evil-doers of Ellsworth looked upon him with wholesome respect, and the killing of nine men was all that was necessary to show them that Bill was master of the situation. After acting as marshal of Ellsworth for a year, Bill decided to make a change, and leaving the town went to Kansas City, Missouri. Here he met and married Mrs. Lake, the widow of a prominent circus-man.

Texans brought many race ponies with them to Abeline and raced them for large sums of money. In those days the distance was one-fourth mile. They started them with their rear to the outcome, and at the crack of a six-shooter fired by the starter, they whirled on their hind legs and ran for dear life to the outcome. I have seen fifty head of Texas steers driven to the race and bet against money on the result. Everyone joined in these poney races. Gamblers, saloonkeepers, cattlemen, cow punchers, dance hall keepers and dance hall girls all bet their money on the results.

In the Summer of 1870 I left Abilene, going to Ellsworth, where I remained until Fall; finally joining the Toole Brothers, who had purchased out of the various herds, eight hundred head of young stock cattle, our destination being Montana.

They intended to winter the cattle on the Arkansas River, about one hundred and twenty-five miles west of Fort Dodge. We arrived there in due time without any trouble, except from the buffalo, which stampeded the cattle two or three times. There were hundreds of thousands of buffalo in the country at this time. After locating ourselves on our winter's range, we built two dug-outs in which to live. These were constructed by cutting into a bank or hillside to the size desired, then roofing it over with ridge and roof poles, and covering all over with dirt. The front end was built up with sod, an opening being left for the door.

One night during the first week we lived in the dug-out, we were awakened by one of the cattle walking over the roof. Before many minutes had elapsed, she fell through up to her body and we experienced a great difficulty in getting her out. Had she fallen all the way down, or through, she would have landed on my bunk, with probably fatal results to both of us.

Our down river dug-out was located nine miles below. Two of the boys and a cook took care of that end of the range. They rode up river every morning and we rode down, meeting them each day and comparing notes. It was necessary to keep the cattle on the range; we also kept two additional men whose duty it was to keep the buffalo off the range; they were called "buffalo whoopers." These buffalo were very destructive to the "buffalo grass." It was very short and curly; always green near the ground and very fattening for stock. The buffalo usually remained in the hills back from the river, where they found numerous large holes, known as "buffalo wallows." These wallows were filled with water from the rains and melting snow, where they procured their drinking water. During the severe winters these holes would freeze over, compelling the buffalo to go to the river for water.

I have heard many controversies regarding the formation of these holes or wallows, and will here explain to you from personal knowledge how they were made and why called buffalo wallows:

During the summer months the buffalo would travel this country in immense herds and were continually attacked by an insect called the buffalo gnat. These gnats would work their way down through the hair into the hide of the buffalo and cause constant itching. In desperation, the buffalo would tear up the earth with his horns and with his front foot throw the loose earth over his body, and then lie down, rolling over and over until his body was completely covered with the earth. This made a depression in the ground. The buffalo would then rise to his feet, shaking his body, causing great clouds of dust which exterminated the gnat. This same performance would be gone through by others until a large, deep hole was the result; thus the name of "buffalo wallow." Thousands of these holes were to be found on the prairie, and were all formed in this manner.

It is wonderful the uses that were made of these buffalo wallows after the buffalo were exterminated, as many a tired emigrant wending his way westward found water for himself and stock; many of them also using these holes as breast works, when attacked by Indians. In the vicinity of these holes was also found a vast amount of offal from the buffalo, called buffalo chips, which was used for fuel for cooking purposes. I, myself, have eaten many a good meal cooked by this kind of fuel.

It was very remarkable, however, that one never found the great buffalo herds moving any direction but south, unless when they were scared, when they would run north for a short distance, but would eventually resume their journey south. It is no exaggeration to say that at times I have stood on heights and have seen hundreds of thousands of these animals in one great herd. The extermination of these vast herds was completed in a few years.

One bright, cold winter morning we were in the dug-out and saw an immense herd of buffalo coming to the river for water.

"Young has never killed a buffalo," said Mr. Toole, when we sighted the herd, "and here is his chance. Let him take the first shot." I took an old Spencer carbine and secreted myself in a clump of willows near the river, in sight of the dug-out. In a few minutes on came the herd and in a short time hundreds of these magnificent animals were on all sides of me. For some reason, however, they did not see or scent me. I became nervous and yelled at them. In a moment everything was in confusion—never shall I forget that grand sight. Every buffalo in the herd seemed to be aware of his danger and immediately stampeded toward the hills. One old bull came within two feet of my hiding place. Although I was very much frightened, I pointed the gun at him and pulled the trigger. I then made a run for the dug-out without waiting to see the result of my shot, completely forgetting that there were other loads in the magazine of the weapon. The buffalo did not immediately fall, although I was sure that my shot had struck him. When near the dug-out I saw the boys looking at a point back of me, and following the direction of their gaze I saw the buffalo in the throes of death. "Why didn't you take another shot at them?" asked Mr. Toole.

"Because," I replied, straightening up as proud as a peacock, "one shot is enough for a green hand." Later on I became quite a buffalo hunter. The four months that I remained with the Toole Brothers, I killed forty-six of these animals. Each herder carried a gun and ammunition, and we were supposed to kill all the buffalo possible; some we used for food, but our principal revenue was from their hides. The prices were three dollars and ten cents for bull hides, and two dollars and ten cents for cow hides. Mr. Toole told me afterward that during their winter stay there, they had killed and sold enough hides to pay the wages and expenses of the men for the entire winter. The almost complete extermination of the buffalo was caused by professional hunters, who were continually killing them for their hides. These hides were hauled to the nearest railroad station, where they were sold and later on shipped to England, where they were made into belting for machinery. Few

were made into buffalo robes, as the hunters did not
have the time to tan them.

To give the reader some idea of the money made
by some of these profession hunters, I will select
one man whom I knew well. His name was Kirt
Jordan. Kirt had three four-horse teams and twenty
men in his employ and was one of the most successful
hunters at this time. He held the record, having
killed a hundred buffalo in one stand. In getting a
stand of buffalo, the hunter must crawl up unawares
without being seen or scented. Should the hunter be
fortunate enough not to be seen or scented, he could
kill numbers of them before they would get out of
gun-shot, as they are not easily frightened. After
quitting the Toole Brothers, I went skinning buffalo
for Kirk Jordan and was the first to suggest and put
into practical operation the skinning of buffalo by
mule power. This was done by cutting the hide
around the neck, down the belly and up the legs,
after which the skin was started a little. A large
sharp steel pin was then driven through the buffalo's
nose and into the ground; then a hole was cut in
the back part of the hide at the neck, a chain hooked
in the cut and by means of a collar, hames, traces and
single-tree, with which the mule was equipped, the
hide was pulled off the buffalo with the greatest of
ease. Of course, by this operation much of the flesh
adhered to the hide, but the market value of the latter
was not affected in the least. After the hides had
been staked out until partly dry, they were loaded on
wagons, which were equipped with a rack similar
to a hay-rack, also using a binding pole. In this
way a great many hides could be hauled in one load.
These wagons were drawn by four animals to the
nearest town on the line of the Atchison, Topeka &
Santa Fe railroad, and sold at the prices previously
mentioned. Anyone who was a good hunter and who
had an outfit, could make a great deal of money in

this business as long as it lasted. Kirk Jordan made thousands of dollars.

Kirt Jordan, the great buffalo hunter, finally went wrong, and became a horse and mule thief. The U. S. marshal arrested him for stealing government mules, tried and sentenced him to Leavenworth Government Prison for ten years. An officer and two men, with Kirt handcuffed, started for Leavenworth, Kirt sitting in the seat with the officer, and the soldiers sitting in the seat at his back. Kirt requested the officer to unhandcuff him as he wished to wash himself in the toilet. The officer did so, when, as quick as lightning, he grabbed the officer's six-shooter from his scabard and shot him dead. He then shot one of the soldiers, and jumped through the open window to the ground, lighting on his head and breaking his neck. Poor Kirt was a good fellow, but, like many others, after his occupation as a buffalo hunter ended, he could not resume his occupation as a teamster, and accordingly went bad.

Billie Brooks, the gun man of Dodge City in the early seventies, was one day riding on the construction train from Dodge City to Sergeant. The conductor, coming through the coach, asked him for his fare. Brooks replied by drawing his six-shooter, saying, "I travel on this." The conductor passed on. After he was through with his fare collecting, he went forward to the locomotive and instructed the engineer to slow down at a certain point. Getting his shotgun, he dropped off the engine and caught the last car, in which Brooks was seated. Approaching from the back, he called out, "Brooks, the fare to Sergeant is $2.75." Brooks looked over his shoulder, and seeing the shotgun pointed at him, replied:

"To whom do I pay the money?"

Just then the brakeman stepped in. The conductor said, "Pay the brakeman, and also hand him your six-shooters, and when you arrive at Sergeant the agent there will return them to you."

Brooks did so. Meeting the conductor the same night in the dance hall, Brooks said, "Old man, you are a good fellow and a good collector, and I want to be your friend." Thus the matter ended.

Brooks in future days became a horse and mule thief, and was chased by a posse to a dugout near Wichita, where he stood the posse off for two days. He was finally induced to surrender with the promise that he would be tried by law in Wichita. He was told to leave his guns in the dugout and walk out unarmed. He did so, and was mounted on a horse and taken to a nearby tree and hanged. Thus ended Brooks' career as a gun man.

One year after the Santa Fe railroad had been constructed along the Arkansas river, there came into that country an old man with a two-horse team, who quietly began the gathering of buffalo bones, hauling them to the railroad and piling them in great heaps. The boys all laughed at him and dubbed him "Old Buffalo Bones." The old fellow enjoyed their joking him and kept on with his gathering. Later he procured another team and sent east for his son to drive it. The following year this man had many great piles of bones ready for shipment east. The Santa Fe railroad being anxious to load their empty cars eastward, gave him a very low rate and laid sidetracks to the piles. The records at Dodge City show that this "Old Bones" shipped three thousand carloads to Philadalphia, where they were used in sugar refineries and for fertilizing purposes. This old man, at whom we had laughed, made a great fortune in two years.

To give the reader an idea of the number of buffalo killed in that country, the railroad records at Dodge

City show that two million buffalo hides were shipped from that station alone, and it is estimated that there were twenty-million buffalo killed between the boundaries of Montana and Texas.

CHAPTER VII.

STRENUOUS PIONEER LIFE AT FORT DODGE—UNSUNG
AND UNHUNG HEROES—BOOT HILL CEMETERY—
PORTABLE DANCE HALLS—CARNIVAL OF MURDER
—WORK OF THE VIGILANTES—THE FAITHFUL
BULLDOG—HORRIBLE PRACTICAL JOKE ON THE
BUFFALO SKIN ROBBER—"RUN, DARCY! RUN FOR
LIFE"—TRIBUTE TO THE DANCE HALL GIRL.

IN the early spring of 1871, having tired of the
buffalo skinning business, I returned to the
Atchison, Topeka & Santa Fe extension, that I
might experience frontier life, then to be found in
all its glory. I went over to Dodge City, then the
terminus. The town was two miles west of Fort Dodge
and all the elements of frontier life were there, including many saloons and three large dance halls. That the
town was rough, goes without question. Buffalo
hunters made their headquarters here, and disposed
of their hides and spent their money lavishly.

. There are few who know, and it is difficult to con-
ceive, how hardened men can become when in such
surroundings as existed there. My experiences in
that town were many and varied, and the characters
were a study for one of a contemplative turn of mind.
Among those whom I now recall were Billy Brooks,
of Newton fame; "Dog" Kelly, who kept a large saloon
there and who derived his nicname "Dog" from being
a large owner of greyhounds, which the sporting
element used for hunting jack rabbits. They bet a
great deal of money on these hounds and made very
fine sport of it. I understand that this character,
Kelly, is still alive in Dodge City. Other characters,
Pete Hicks, who was day marshal; his brother Bill,
night marshal, and both of whom were killed there
later on, and Bat Masterson, who is now living in

New York. Others were, Lushy Bill, Ed. Hurley, Fancy Pat, Tom Sherman, Mose Walters, Jim Hannafan, Joe Hunt, George Peacock, and many whose names I have forgotten. At this particular time in the west, a great many men had nicknames and one never did know their proper names and cared less.

As an illustration of the lawlessness in that town: One night Ed. Hurley and three others were crossing from the main town to the dance-hall. They saw a buffalo hunter standing in the middle of the street, yelling at the top of his voice: "I am a wolf, it is my night to howl, and I would like to have some —— —— stop me."

"What is the matter with you?" asked Hurley, walking up to the fellow.

"I am a wolf," was the reply; "it is my night to howl and the whole bunch of you can't stop me."

Whereupon, Hurley, without a word of warning, shot him dead. Hurley then kicked him, saying as he did so: "Now, why don't you howl?" Hurley then went on to the dance-hall, singing as he did so. As he entered the door, he saw a man named McClelland talking to a dance-hall girl named Nellie Rivers. This aroused Hurley's jealousy, and he began shooting at McClelland; the latter returning the fire, killed Hurley. McClelland at this time was a brakesman on the railroad, but after this episode, he left the job and became a gun-fighter. His career was short, however, for he was killed by a desperado named "Scotty" in Peacock's saloon just one week after he killed Hurley. After the killing, McClelland lay on the bar room floor when Nellie Rivers, who had heard of his death, came in to look at him. Sitting astride of his body, folding his hands over his breast, she cried "you killed my Eddie! You killed my Eddie!" meaning Hurley; emphasizing the statement each time by slapping the face of the dead man. She continued slapping him and finally had to be pulled away.

McClelland was buried the next morning in Boot Hill cemetery, the name "Boot Hill' being acquired from the fact that all who were buried there had died with their boots on. The one exception was a drunken painter who had died of delerium tremens. This cemetery is still a landmark of early days, and during the six months that I lived in Dodge, sixty-five men were buried there, all having died "with their boots on."

At this time I was night watchman at the Government freight shed, situated at the east limit of the town. Although, I will confess, instead of remaining on duty at night as I should have done, I spent a great portion of my time in the dance-halls. One beautiful moonlight night, I, together with about one hundred others, was in one of these places, when a drunken buffalo hunter stepped in at the door and exclaiming, "Oh, what a field," began shooting over our heads. He did not cease shooting until he had emptied both guns. When the dance-hall was built, it was made up in sections, fastened together with hooks and staples, so that when the towns moved on ·farther west, the hall could be loaded on flat cars and set up again at the next terminus. When the drunken hunter began shooting, the crowd made its escape by rushing head-long against the sides of the hall, practically knocking the structure to pieces. We all made our escape and as no one was hit, it is my belief that he shot only to frighten us. The citizens, however, could not see the situation in that light and advocated hanging, as the best remedy.

They probably thought that one might as well be killed as almost scared to death, and for this reason they failed to see the point of the joke and insisted on hanging him. He ran up into one of the canyons near the town, but was caught later and brought back. He was tried in "Dog Kelly's saloon, convicted and taken out to be hanged. He broke away and ran for his wagon, which was on the edge of the town, and as he crawled under it, he was shot by Pete Hicks, the marshal. His faithful bulldog was tied under the wagon and when one of the men reached to pull the dead body out, the dog seized him by the arm and had to be killed before he would let go.

One of the closest calls I ever had was in Dodge City. I was in "Handsome Harry's" saloon one day and had some difficulty with a cook who worked in the restaurant next door, when a few blows were exchanged. He went away, and I supposed the trouble was over. A little later on, I was standing at the bar with my back toward the entrance of the saloon when he entered, and without any warning took two shots at me; neither one taking effect. I being unarmed, one of the crowd caught and held him until I could get my gun, which happened to be behind the bar. We then agreed to go out on the prairie and settle the matter. We were to place our backs together, walk ten paces in opposite directions, turn and fire. We went out, but before either of us could do any damage, our friends interefered and the proceedings stopped. It is probable that neither of us regretted the interference very much, for later we became warm friends. He and another man went south a few weeks later to sell whiskey to the Kiwa Indians. Unfortunately, arriving in their country while they were on the war path, it resulted in the cook and his partner being killed by this tribe and all their whiskey being confiscated.

The town of Dodge City soon afterward became so tough that the saloon men and merchants formed themselves into a vigilance committee and appointed Fancy Pat as their leader. They were determined to rid the town of all undesirable characters. Equipping themselves with revolvers, rifles and shot-guns, they made ready for the slaughter. Selecting all the tough men whom they wished to exterminate, at a given signal they swooped on all three dance-halls and began shooting—and what a slaughter. Fourteen men were killed and were left lying in the street all night where they fell. I recollect the name of only one of the victims, "Tex Williams." Tex was shot completely to pieces, as he ran out of the front door of the dance-hall. He was a ghastly sight, being riddled from head to foot. I was told later that even small screws were picked out of his body. I do not doubt the truth of this assertion, as many of the men used small screws as ammunition for their shot-guns. At the time of the killing, I was standing in a saloon, when two or three of the men, whom the Regulators were after, ran through the room and secreted themselves in the coal cellar. The Regulators came in shortly and asked Frank Pedrie, the bar-keeper, if any of the gang were hidden thereabouts. Pedrie replied "No," when they took a drink all round, and left for Sherman's dance-hall. They then collected all the dance-hall girls, who had run away screaming when the shooting took place. One of the dead men lay in front of the entrance to the hall, where he had dropped when shot.

It was a cold, in fact, freezing night, and as he lay there with wide open mouth, his eyes set in death, and his body entirely covered with blood, he was a sight to sicken the strongest. One of the dance-hall girls tied her handkerchief around his head to keep his mouth closed, when one of the Regulators, who witnessed this humane act, struck her on the head with his six-shooter, wounding her severely. The dead body of the victim lay there until daylight, while the Regulators enjoyed themselves dancing and drinking. It was an awful night of murder and carnage.

I say murder, for most all the Regulators were themselves gun-fighters as well as businessmen, and many
of them were equally as bad as their victims.

The morning after the killing they employed six
carpenters, who made seven boxes out of rough lumber, putting two victims in each box, then loading
them onto two-horse wagons. The procession then
started for Boot Hill cemetery—and such a sight!
I shall never forget it. Most everyone in town turned
out, the greatest part of whom were the Regulators,
who had done the killing. They had caroused all night,
some shooting as they proceeded up the hill; others
laughing, and others swearing. Each man linked arms
with a dance-hall girl. Finally arriving at the prepared graves, they lowered each box and made all
kinds of gestures and remarks.

While the earth was shoveled onto the boxes, they
circled around, dancing like a lot of wild Indians.
One of them, I recollect, remarked, "Let us give
them each a flask of whiskey, to use on their way to
hell." Work was stopped until the seven flasks of
whiskey were procured and deposited in the graves,
when all returned to town, yelling and laughing. This
ended the night of horror in Dodge City, Kansas.

Shortly after this occurrence took place, complaint
was made by the buffalo hide merchants that someone
was stealing their hides, which were piled up in the
streets in front of their stores. Five hundred dollars
reward was finally offered for the capture of the
thieves. I was asked by the Hicks Brothers to assist
them in capturing the guilty parties. While on watch
one moonlight night, we saw a man getting away
with two hides on his shoulder. We called on him to
halt, but instead of obeying us, he dropped the hides
and ran. We took a shot at him but missed and he
continued running toward the Arkansas river, and we
following him. When he had run into the water up to

his waist, he threw up his hands and promised to come out if we would not shoot. On his return to the bank we discovered that it was Darcey, one of the town's old drunks. He begged to be allowed to go, as he was only trying to get a little money with which to buy whiskey. I favored letting him go and saying nothing of the occurrence. But the Hicks Brothers wanted that five hundred dollars blood money, and insisted that he be summarily dealt with. We took him to the railroad station and reported the capture to the merchants. When they saw who it was, they decided to release him. Dog Kelly, however, saw an opportunity for a practical joke, and had poor old Darcey brought up to his saloon and tried for the offense. Of course, he was found guilty; the verdict was that he should be hanged to a telegraph pole. The old man begged and prayed for mercy, but without avail. He was taken up the railroad track and while one of the men was climbing the pole to arrange the rope, Kelly, according to a prearranged plan, whispered to Darcey, "Now is your chance; run for your life." The old fellow taking advantage of the opportunity began to run as he had never run before. Suddenly we began shooting in the air and yelling "Stop Darcey! Stop!" we running after him. Of course, we stopped after a little and allowed him to escape. He probably considered it the closest call of his life; and I think, if alive, he is running yet, as he was never again seen in that vicinity.

I wish to make special mention of the class of dance-hall girls that were brought to Dodge City in early days. In many instances they were girls who had been well raised, but who were inveigled into that tough town by misrepresentation on the part of whom we would term today "Whiteslavers." After getting them to Dodge, they would put them in dance-halls, turning them over to gun-men who became their lovers and by whom they were treated in nearly all cases most cruelly. Nellie Rivers, of whom I have spoken, was well educated and very handsome, and evidently came from a good family. Realizing the unavoidable position in which she was placed and the hopelessness of ever getting back to her former home, she became a great hater of men and seemed possessed of a mania for having them killed for trivial reasons. After succeeding in being the cause of having five killed, she was considered so dangerous that it was decided to hang her. Her life was saved, however, through the intervention of Fancy Pat and Dog Kelly. She was allowed to leave town with the understanding that she was not to return. She was never again seen in her old haunts.

Many of these dance-hall girls had rough exteriors, which covered warm hearts. One would be surprised at the sacrifices and attentions they would devote to the sick and wounded. I have known many cases where they would quit their work and sit up with them, devoting tender care, and not asking or expecting anything in return. I shall always have a warm spot in my heart for the poor unfortunate dance-hall girls.

It is not generally known at this date that the dance hall girl was the true pioneer woman of the West. Few of them in the seventies, if they stood the stormy days, married good men—cattle men, merchandising men, miners, etc., and made noble wives and mothers. I could name one who bore two sons and one daughter. One of the sons later represented a Middle Western state in the U. S. Congress. After the dance hall girl came the farmer and his wife. Then the dance hall girl disappeared, her occupation being a thing of the past.

It is a true saying that "music hath charms to soothe the savage." I distinctly remember one night in Tom Sherman's dance-hall, when revelry was at its

height; with all its drinking, cursing and swearing.
The revellers were at the bar, each accompanied by
his girl, when suddenly a character named "Sims"
the violinist of the dance-hall, stringing his instru-
ment to a high key, commenced playing in a masterly
style, the old familiar tune "Home, Sweet Home." In
a moment all was still, many holding their liquor
glasses in their hands, their heads bowed and tears
trickling down their cheeks. This was a very unusual scene, and one never to be forgotten. Suddenly,
in a loud tone of voice, the dance-hall manager or
more commonly known as the "Bouncer," shouted,
"Get your partners for the next quadrille." All was
forgotten; the music started up and the wild revelry
again resumed. Such was life in the west in early
days. A few words of explanation regarding gun-
fighters of Dodge City and other frontier towns.
Take such men as Bat Masterson: he was the soul of
honor and only killed when it was necessary to protect himself. Luke Short, who had a great reputation
as a gun-man, followed the occupation of a gambler
and killed many men. Luke was a fine man, with
gentlemanly instincts, but quick tempered. He was
considered square and much respected; also Wyat
Erap, who had considerable trouble in Arizona in
early days, and killed with his brothers many men
in that country. I met Wyat in Nome, Alaska, in
1900 and found him a perfect gentleman. This class
of men didn't kill for gain. Another class of gun-
men who were desperadoes, horse thieves and road
agents, who killed for gain. This class were entirely
different from Masterson, Short and Earp.

CHAPTER VIII.

MURDERS FOR MONEY—TWO INNOCENT MEN SUFFER
FOR THE CRIME—THE FACTS ONLY RECENTLY
TOLD—CATCHING BUFFALO—OVER TO THE UNION
PACIFIC RAILROAD — WILD BILL AGAIN — "RED
PAT," THE TEAMSTER, WHO STILL LIVES.

ANOTHER tough character at Dodge City, was
"Kelly the Rake." While I was herding
cattle for Toole Brothers, Kelly and another
tough denizen named Red Johnson, whom I
had met in Wichita, entered the employ of a
man named Jack (I do not recollect his other name);
they camped at our upper dug-out. These three men,
Kelly, Johnson and Jack, were going southward for
the purpose of hunting buffalo, forming a partnership
for that purpose. Sometime later Johnson and Kelly
returned to the town of Sergeant, on the Colorado-
Kansas state line, and at that time the terminus
of the A. T. & S. F. Ry. They returned with a big
load of buffalo hides and the information that they
had bought out the third man, Jack. The hides were
sold to Chris Gillson, after which Johnson and Kelly
became gloriously drunk. While in this condition they
met Clark and McClellan, two buffalo skinners who
were in town and to whom they imparted the information that they, Kelly and Johnson, had killed Jack
and buried him in the sand hills. On sobering up
the next day, they became alarmed lest Clark and
McClellan should divulge what had been told them.
Determined to put these men out of the way, if
possible, Kelly and Johnson went to Chris Gillson and
told him that Clark and McClellan were planning to
kill and rob him that night. Gillson, who had just
received a large sum of money from the sale of a lot
of hides, was very much alarmed and spent the night

in a box car instead of in his tent. The next morning
Chris and I were standing outside his tent, talking,
when Clark and McClellan came along, with no
thought of danger. Chris, who had a doubled-barreled
shotgun in his hands, emptied one barrel of the
weapon into Clark, killing him instantly. He then
pursued McClellan, who was by this time attempting
to get away, and shot him down, the poor fellow
begging all the time for mercy.

The reader will possibly question the source of
my information regarding this affair. I did not come
into possession of the facts in the case until several
years later, when I was employed as traveling passenger agent for the Oregon Railroad & Navigation
Company, and on one occasion had to go to St. Paul,
Minn., stopping off en route at every coupon ticket
office on the line of the Northern Pacific Railway.
Shortly after leaving Miles City, Montana, I went into
the smoking car. There I noticed a pock-marked man
sitting in front of me and whose face seemed familiar.
Presently, I realized who he was. "How are you
Chris?" I asked, turning to him.

"You have the best of me," was his reply. "What
is your name?" On being told who I was, he showed
great delight, and together we spent some time talking over the old days on the A. T. & S. F.

"Have you ever seen 'Kelly the Rake' in your
travels?" he asked. I told him no.

"Well," he continued, "if I ever meet him, he will
be a dead man." After which he told me the story
narrated above. He also told me he had found out
in the intervening time that McClellan and Clark were
innocent of any intention to injure him, and that
Kelly had maliciously told him this story for his own
protection, with the thought in mind that "dead men
tell no tales."

Chris was on his way to Washington, D. C., to collect some Government money due him for two years' surveying work done in Alaska. I have not seen him since we met that day.

A few days after this occurred at Sergeant, four of us went down river to a ranch kept by a man named "Prairie Dog Dave," for the purpose of catching buffalo calves, our intention being to ship them east by rail. Insofar as our catching the calves was concerned, we were very successful. They were caught in the following manner:

Mounted on our horses, we got as near the herd as possible, unseen, then suddenly riding after them. The cows and young calves, when the herd was stampeded would naturally drop to the rear and the cows would remain with the calves until closely pressed, when they would desert them. We would then jump from our horses, throw the calves down and tie their legs.

At ths season of the year, the calves were about two months old. We succeeded in catching twenty head, and finally hauled them to the ranch by wagon. However, we soon discovered that we could not tame them, nor could we get them to eat, so out of pity we let them go. Before doing so, however, two were drowned in a spring near the ranch. We had picketed them out, taking the ends of a lariat and fastening it around their necks, then taking the middle of the lariat and attaching it to a picket pin, which we drove into the ground, but the poor little fellows became entangled in it and fell into the spring, where they were drowned. Two others escaped with a sixty foot lariat, which we never recovered, and I shall always believe that someone stole the lariat and allowed the calves to get away. Our venture was not a success. We became discouraged and gave up the business.

Had I known as much in those days as I do at the present time, I could have made a fortune buying buffalo robes, trading with the Indians, who had thousands of them and which would not have cost to exceed five dollars each in trade. A buffalo robe today is worth from one hundred to five hundred dollars.

I left this section of the country in the fall of 1871, going to Pueblo, Colorado, from which place I went to Denver, Colorado. Here I worked for a short time and then went to Cheyenne, Wyoming,— situated on the Union Pacific railroad. There I resumed my old occupation as a "six-mule skinner" for the Government, driving out of Camp Carlin, which was then the Government supply station for all northern posts. It was located between Cheyenne and Fort D. A. Russell, on the Union Pacific railroad. I remained there for about a year.

One night in Cheyenne I strolled into McDaniels' variety show. On entering the door I spied my old friend "Wild Bill" standing with his back to the wall, looking on at a faro game. He did not look very prosperous, and I was quite sure that the world had been treating him badly since I had last seen him, or he certainly would have been one of the players. I also noticed that when he sat down, he kept the cases. This gave him an opportunity to pick up any sleepers that might be left on any dead card by an inexperienced player.

On seeing me, Bill remarked in a pleased tone: "Hello, Kid! I am glad to see you. Where have you been for the last few years, and how is the world treating you?"

I told him what I had been doing and also what I was doing at that time. He finally told me that he was broke.

This particular night, a man named Ed O'Malley was playing the game, and leaving a bet on the jack, which had become dead, Bill naturally reached over and took the checks. Later, O'Malley, missing his checks, inquired of the dealer what became of his bet on the jack. The dealer did not answer him, but some man among the players whispered to him that Wild Bill took it, whereupon O'Malley rushed up to Bill, and with a string of expletives, demanded that Bill replace the checks on the table. Bill looked up at him, saying, "What would you do if I did not replace them?"

O'Malley replied, "I would cut your heart out."

Bill smiled and then said, "Then I had better replace them;" which he did. This O'Malley, whose occupation was that of a camp cook, was a fighting Irishman and had killed a man several months prior by stabbing him with a carving knife.

There are many persons who entertain the idea that Wild Bill was noisy and quarrelsome, but this impression is not at all correct. During the years of my acquaintance with him, I never knew him to pick a quarrel, but have known him to stop many that might have ended seriously.

At this time a man named Jeff Carr was marshal of Cheyenne, and when Bill arrived there Carr went to him, saying: "You can remain in this town as long as you wish by giving me your word of honor that you will not carry your gun on your person, nor get into any trouble that you can possibly avoid." Bill agreed to these terms, with one proviso namely, that he be allowed to put his gun within easy reach in any house that he might be. As an illustration, when he came into McDaniels' theatre, he put his gun behind the bar.

While in Cheyenne, Bill had won the affections of a girl whoes lover was a man named "Fighting Tom" and who was the night marshal of the town. Tom recognized in Bill a dangerous rival and to get him out of the way, assumed the responsibility of ordering Bill to leave town within twenty-four hours.

"Why should I leave town?" Bill asked. "Furthermore, by whose orders are you attempting to run me out?"

"By order of Jeff Carr," was Tom's reply. Without further to do, Bill went up to Carr's house and asked him why he had ordered him out of town. Carr was much surprised at the question, and said he knew nothing about the matter. Bill then told Carr what Fighting Tom had said. To this Carr replied: "You may remain in this town as long as you please, so long as you keep your word given to me." Upon this Bill returned to the variety show and calling Tom aside, said to him: "Tom you have lied to me. Jeff Carr says so and I say so. Now if you ever look my way while I am in Cheyenne, there will be a vacancy in this town for a night marshal." Tom made no reply, but walked away, and thus ended the matter.

Cheyenne in those days was a very lively town. The Union Pacific had their railroad shop there. Fort D. A. Russell was a very large post, having a great many soldiers in it. Camp Carlin was also a large place, and a great many teamsters were employed there. All the freighting to northern posts,—Fort Laramie, Fort Fetterman and others, originated from Cheyenne. The reader can imagine what pay day meant at Fort D. A. Russell, where at least one thousand soldiers were paid on the same day; one hundred teamsters would also be paid at Camp Carlin. In addition to this was the railroad employees' pay day. This naturally circulated a great deal of money. The town had many saloons, gambling houses and dance-halls, with its quota of gamblers and dance-hall girls, and I assure you it was a very live town. Many of the merchants and business men were ex-government teamsters or soldiers, who had been discharged from the army. For instance, Mr. H. E. Post was formerly a teamster, but at this time postmatser, and later represented Cheyenne in United States congress.

One of the largest saloons in Cheyenne was kept by a character named Red Pat,—so dubbed because of the color of his hair. This fellow was an ex-teamster and his saloon was the great resort for the mule-skinners. While in his place we would spend our money like drunken sailors, and when we were broke, he would give us a few dollars and tell us to go hunt another job. Pat was a good old soul, but a bad man in a rough and tumble fight. I learned recently that he is still alive and doing business at the same old location.

To give the reader some idea of Cheyenne on Government pay-day, the citizens would send all kinds of vehicles out to the Fort and Camp Carlin, taking us into town free of charge. Jeff Carr, the marshal, would deputize twenty-five extra men to keep some semblance of order. They were not severe, however, and I have seen them when a couple of soldiers were fighting, keep the crowd back by forming a ring, letting the contestants fight it out. Just as long as the soldiers or mule-skinners had money to spend, they tolerated them, but as soon as their money was gone, they then began to drive them out of town, and in some cases, clubbed them unmercifully. We went back to our jobs, swearing that next pay-day we would not go into Cheyenne, but we would invariably land there the following pay-day. At the time I drove a team at Camp Carlin. Our superintendent was a man named Botsford, of whom I will write later on.

CHAPTER IX.

ON THE CHUGWATER—DEAR OLD FORT LARAMIE—A
TEAMSTER JOB WITH ROUGH ATTACHMENTS—MY
FIRST SIOUX — PLENTY MORE — TWENTY MILES
ALONE AND UNARMED—ON WHITE RIVER—RED
CLOUD—LIBERALITY EXPLAINED.

IN the summer of 1872, I quit my job as teamster
and went to the ranch of Jack Hunton, located on
a stream called the Chugwater, where I worked
with his brother Jim, getting out fence posts,
about two miles from the river, at a place called
Goshen Hole. Some two years after this the Sioux
Indians killed and scalped Jim while he was hunting
for stock. After quitting Hunton, I went to Fort Laramie. There I applied for a position as teamster, but
as there was no vacancy, I could not get employment.

I wish the reader to understand that I had not as
yet met any bad wild Indians. However, this experience came to me before I had been in Laramie many
days. Hearing that Cuney & Coffee wanted a teamster at their ranch, four miles up the Laramie river,
I went there that evening and applied for the job.
Cuney informed me that he did want a teamster. He
then asked me to have a drink, and after talking a
while, he said: "We pay forty dollars a month and
board to drivers of our four-mule teams, and you may
go to work tomorrow morning. Now enjoy yourself."
I informed him that I could not afford to blow myself,
as my money was limited. "Drink all you want;" was
his reply, "there are no charges to a new-comer."
I looked upon his open-heartedness with suspicion, but
took a few drinks, after which I fell asleep.

Jack Bowman, the bartender, took me into a side
room filled with furs of all descriptions and I lay there
and slept until Jack wakened me about daylight. He

then gave me a bottle of mustard pickles and some crackers, for the purpose, he said, of settling my stomach. They surely did. Jack told me that my team was hitched up outside and ready to start. I thought him one of the best fellows I had ever met.

"Now," said Jack, "you are to take this load of canned goods to Mr. Deere, a trader on White River, two hundred miles north of here. This," he added, handing me a piece of paper, on which was written the miles, camps, rivers, etc., of the road, "is a memorandum of stopping and camping places." Off I started, all alone—no gun or other means of protection, only food for the mules and myself. I made my noon and night camps without any trouble, cooked my supper and staked out the mules, after which I rolled up in my blankets and slept like a log for the remainder of the night.

Next morning I missed the mules, and later found that they had pulled up their stakes and started back home. Immediately after breakfast, I went back after them and found them at the spring where I had camped the noon of the preceding day. Catching one and mounting him, I drove the other three back to my wagon, arriving there about sundown. There, standing by my wagon, and with his back to the fire, was a sure-enough, real, live Indian—flaming colors, blanket, moccasins and all. He was the genuine article; the first real wild Indian I had ever seen. He was a Sioux.

"How, how!" was his salutation, as I walked up to the wagon.

"How are you?" I replied. Whereupon he made signs indicating that he wanted me to cook him some supper, which I did. I performed all the work, he making no move to help me. When supper was over he went up on a knoll and remained there until dark, after which he returned and got into bed with me.

As I was all alone, I was certainly glad I met the Sioux and hoped he would continue the journey with me. We talked together for some time, but neither one could make the other understand, and we finally gave it up as a bad job.

He was up before me in the morning, and back on that knoll, where he remained until breakfast was ready. When the meal had been prepared, he came down and ate with me, after which he went back again and took his station on the knoll. "You are a whole lot of help to me, you are, you big, lazy loafer," was my mental comment.

Presently I hitched up and started, when, much to my delight, he crawled up onto the wagon, as though intending to accompany me on my journey. He then began making signs which I interpreted as wanting to know whether or not I had a gun in the wagon. I shook my head, at which he seemed much surprised, and inclined to doubt my word. He then began to search the wagon, all the while making signs about the gun. After my repeated efforts to convince him, he seemed satisfied that I was telling the truth and lay down in the wagon.

That night we camped again, he, as usual, going out on a high point for a while. Finally coming in and sleeping with me again. This program was repeated every day for five days. Just before sundown of the sixth evening, we were stopped by about fifty or sixty of the wildest looking Indians I ever saw, many of whom had not enough clothing on to flag a handcar. My Indian friend, who was in the wagon with me, began to talk Sioux to them in an excited manner, but, of course, I had not the remotest idea what they were talking about. In a few moments they left suddenly, after which my companion motioned excitedly for me to go on. This I was loath to do, as we were about to go into camp for the night, but he kept making signs for me to hurry on, at the same time putting his hand on my head, strongly suggesting the scalp act.

I thought the heathen had gone crazy. In a minute or two he blurted out, "Pawnee heap shoot!" But still I was simpleton enough not to know what he meant. However, I started on and he kept me moving until midnight. I was very much frightened by his actions, as I hadn't the slightest idea why he was so excited. When the night was half gone, a number of camp fires loomed up in the distance ahead, at which my Indian friend seemed much relieved. He then left me suddenly, without any ceremony. Seeing a haystack, I pulled up to it, where I unhitched my tired and hungry mules, after which I then turned in for a little sleep.

The first thing I heard the next morning was a white man saying, "young feller, if you don't watch your harness pretty sharp, you won't have a strap left when these Indians get around you. They will steal every inch of it." I stared about me in surprise, and to my astonishment saw a great many Indian lodges and hundreds of Indians, including squaws and papooses. "Is this Deere's Trading Post?" I asked.

"Yes," was the reply, "this is Deere's Trading Post, for the Sioux Indians, at the Red Cloud Agency. Who are you, and where are you from, and how did you get here?" On being informed that I had come from Cuney & Coffee's ranch, he manifested great surprise. "Where are the other teams?" he asked.

"There are no other teams that I know of," was my reply.

"Do you mean to tell me that you came alone from the ranch of Cuney & Coffee to this place?" he interrogated.

"Certainly; my only companion was an Indian whom I picked up on the road, and who has just left me, or rather, when I got in here last night."

"Come with me," he said. And he took me into Deer's store near by. "Deere, here is a tenderfoot who came all alone from Cuney & Coffee's ranch with your load of canned goods."

"Great Caesar!" exclaimed Deere. "Haven't you a gun?"

"No," I replied.

"Well," was the rejoiner, "they certainly played you a dirty trick sending you here all alone, and the only thing that saved you was having that Indian with you, whom you picked up." Still, I could not understand how the Indian had figured in my safety. The men around the camp tried all day to find the Indian who rode with me, but did not succeed in doing so.

I was quite favorably impressed with Red Cloud Agency. It was in its infancy but beginning to assume large proportions. The surroundings were novel to me and I quickly came to the conclusion that if I could secure work here, I would much prefer it to my present job with Cuney & Coffee. Accordingly, I asked Dr. Seville, who was the agent, if he could use me as a laborer. He replied, "Yes, but you must first return Cuney & Coffee's team to them." I lost little time in preparing for my journey back to Fort Laramie and was taken by surprise when Ben Tibbetts, the man who had awakened me upon my arrival, asked me where I was going. I told him and he replied: "You fool. Don't you know that by going alone you would never reach the ranch? Wait here my boy; there are other teams going very soon and the men will not only be company for you, but protection too." He also loaned me a six-shooter, which I was to return to him when I got back to the Agency.

After waiting a few days, I left in company with eight other teams, two of which belonged to the Agency and one to a Mr. Jones, who had lived among the Sioux for years and who was well acquainted with their habits and mode of life. The first night out we camped in some high willows on the bank of a stream called "Running Water." After eating supper we were sitting around the campfire, when suddenly the willows began to crash, and much to our surprise fifty mounted Indians appeared on the scene. My first thought was to jump away from the campfire. This I did. In doing so, I drew my six-shooter and when I came to my senses, as I had been badly frightened, I was pointing my six-shooter at an Indian who was mounted, but I had neglected to pull the trigger. I am glad I did not shoot, as we soon ascertained that they did not intend to harm us. Mr. Jones spoke to them in Sioux and was told that they were acting as an escort to Joe Bessnet, a half-breed, who was carrying the Government mail to the agency. In a little while Bessnet showed up, accompanied by more Indians. They then took supper and went their way, singing one of their war songs.

In our party was a young man named Spencer, who had been continually boasting of his bravery. After the Indians were gone Spencer was missing, and Jones and I went over in the direction of the river to search for him. We found he had secreted himself on a small island in the river and was badly frightened. He had waded almost up to his waist in the water to reach the island. For a long while he refused to leave the island and come back to the camp. Jones finally convinced him that there was no danger and he waded to the bank, a pitiful looking sight. Poor fellow, we joked him unmercifully the remainder of the trip. However, had the Indians intended doing us any harm, he might have been the only one to escape.

Before leaving, Tibbetts instructed me to remain at Fort Laramie and when there was a position at the Agency he would send me word by the agency teamsters.

I got back to Fort Laramie in good shape and turned the team over to Cuney & Coffee and was paid off at the rate of forty dollars a month. It was then that I learned why Bowman, the barkeeper, was so liberal with his whiskey. And I also learned that Mr. Cuney had offered as high as two hundred and fifty dollars to the man who would take that load of canned goods to Deere's store. Old timers living in that country and knowing the dangers, would not attempt the trip even at that price. Bowman's object in supplying me with whiskey, keeping me out of sight and starting me off so early in the morning, was for the purpose of not having me meet these old timers, who would in all probability have warned me of the danger of the undertaking.

I then procured a position, driving a six-mule team for the Government at Fort Laramie. Here I remained until November, 1873.

CHAPTER X.

HISTORIC HAPPENINGS AT AND AROUND FORT LARA-
MIE PRIOR TO AND DURING MY TIME THERE—
CUSTOMS AND HABITS OF ARMY OFFICERS—
FRAUDS PERPETRATED—REMINISCENCES OF
EARLY SETTLERS.

I WILL here dwell briefly on the habits and actions of the army officers, stationed at these frontier posts.

The majority of them were heavy gamblers, hard drinkers, and at times brutal in the extreme. Their gambling was with citizens who had the hay, wood and beef contracts with the Government. If the officers were heavy losers, which was frequently the case, they would give their I. O. U.'s in settlement, but which they never intended to pay, and the citizen never dared to enforce payment, because, on account of their contracts, they were to a certain extent in the clutches of the officers. The Inspection Board was composed of these officers, and the reader can readily understand the position of the citizen contractor with the officer.

I have known many loads of hay to be hauled to Fort Laramie, which had the night before arrival been damped with buckets of water and many shovels of sand to increase the weight. The sand and water would settle through the hay during the jar of the last day's drive. The Inspection Officer would have it probed with an iron rod and the load accepted or rejected, according to the friendly or unfriendly terms with the contractor.

While I was employed at Fort Laramie as a teamster, there was a great fraud exposed regarding approximately three acres of cord wood. In the changing of quartermasters, the detection of this fraud came about. The new quartermaster discovered that while the outside ricks of wood were all right, the inside ricks in numerous cases did not exist at all. The deception consisted of merely laying sticks across the intervening space to each alternate rick, leaving spaces that should have been ricks of wood; thus the Government had been systematically robbed of many thousands of dollars. While the matter was hushed up, I noticed from that time on, the ricks were placed with a space between each to prevent a similar reoccurrence.

Frauds of all descriptions were practiced at all the frontier posts, even the teamsters having their share of the spoils. For instance, a teamster would have an arrangement with the Quartermaster-Sergeant, who had charge of the distribution of the material used by teamsters. The teamster would cut his wagon sheet into four parts, one of which he would take to the sergeant for which he would receive a new wagon sheet in place of the quarter portion; this sheet he would sell to citizen freighters for five dollars. The freighter would cut out the letters "U. S." and fix it up with a patch. Of course, the sergeant received his half of the five dollars.

This would be repeated each day until the teamster had received four new wagon sheets for his old one. Citizens purchased largely from Government employees in this way. All articles had a standard value. Bacon was worth twenty-five cents per pound; shelled corn, two dollars per sack; wall tents, fourteen dollars each; canned tomatoes, fifty cents per can; beans, two dollars per sack, etc., etc. In those days these frauds were not looked upon as a crime. If the fraud was discovered, the guilty ones were black-balled and driven from the reservation.

I will cite one instance of brutality which is on record at the War Department in Washington.

One afternoon I was in close proximity to the cavalry stables, when I heard a man screaming. Running over there, I saw a soldier tied up by the thumbs, and Captain Mix, of M-Company, Second Cavalry standing close by, ordering his first sergeant and another soldier to pull him higher; which they did, until his feet were clear off the floor. The weight being so great, the man's thumbs were pulled from the sockets. The officer of the day, hearing the man yell, ran down to him and seeing his condition ordered him lowered down and removed to the hospital, afterward placing Captain Mix under arrest. Later on, Mix was court-martialed, severely reprimanded, but acquitted, his victim having in the meantime deserted, probably aided by some bribe from Mix. This was what was termed, "whitewashing." However, from this very act some benefit was derived, as the War Department at Washington issued an order abolishing corporal punishment in the United States army.

I wish to impress the reader very forcibly with the importance and usefulness of old Fort Laramie. This post was located at the junction of the Platte and Laramie rivers, one hundred and ten miles north of Cheyenne, Wyoming. It was established previous to 1849. In that year there was a rush of "fortune hunters" to California for gold, and emigrants hailed Fort Laramie as a haven of rest. It was there they received a warm welcome from the citizens, composed mostly of trappers and hunters from the Hudson Bay company; there they made all the repairs to their outfits, shod their horses and oxen, and there was not then nor is there today an emigrant who has not a word of praise and a warm spot in his heart for dear old Fort Laramie.

I have attended reunions of pioneers in Oregon, and it is surprising how many of these old people in telling of their trip across the plains, will mention

Fort Laramie. One would say, "I traded two milch cows that I brought all the way from Missouri, for a pair of horses at Fort Laramie." Another would say, "My oldest boy was born at Fort Laramie;" another, "John Smith was married to Betsy Brown at Fort Laramie," etc., etc.

This post being in the heart of the Sioux country, the emigrants were furnished with military escorts to remain with them until they were well beyond the danger zone. It is a great shame that the United States Government abandoned this post, as it should have remained intact as a great historical center, on the old emigrant trail. It is now owned by Jack Hunton; most of the old buildings have been torn down, or have gone to rack and ruin. Hunton resides there, and I understand is now farming the ground that was formerly the post.

This man Hunton came from Virginia and settled in Wyoming in 1849 and has lived there all these years. I met his brother, Tom, some five years ago, who informed me that Jack was eighty years of age, and in good health. He also told me that Jack kept a diary of all the events occurring in that country, and that his intention was to publish it when he arrived at the age of ninety years. This will be a very valuable book. He engaged in various pursuits, from a pony express rider to a large government contractor, freighter and stock raiser. He is well educated, liberal to a fault and has many friends, and is much beloved by all who know him in Wyoming.

Another character and old timer, who is still alive at the ripe old age of eighty-eight, is a man by the name of Hi Kelly. He also rode pony express in early days, but later became the "Live Stock King" of Wyoming, owning vast herds of cattle with unlimited range and employing large numbers of men. He furnished most of the beef used by the army posts and became very wealthy. Among his holdings was a very noted ranch situated half way between Cheyenne and Fort Laramie. This was known as the Chugwater ranch, being located on a river called Chugwater, so named by the Indians for the following reasons:

In the early days when the buffalo were numerous, the Indians stampeded a large herd of them, which they headed for a bluff two hundred feet high on the bank of this river. Thousands of the buffalo went over the bluff, landing in the river, making a noise as they struck the water—"Chug Chug" and thus the name "Chugwater."

It is a matter of history that the Indians camped at this place for three months, skinning the buffalo, tanning their hides and drying their meat. In passing there on our way to Fort Laramie, many a time we teamsters have walked over to the river and seen thousands of buffalo heads and many bones, which proves that the slaughter was immense. Kelly finally disposed of his holdings to a Scotch syndicate, and is now residing in Denver, Colorado. Like many old timers, Kelly took a Sioux squaw for his wife, white women in those days being very scarce. Unlike the majority of the white men, he married his squaw, raised a large family of children, educated them all, and they are today useful members of society. While I am writing of this great, good man, I will cite one instance of his wonderful loyalty to his friends.

Jack Hunton had received a Government contract for a very large supply of beef and was warmly congratulated by Kelly and others, who had bid for the same contract. Hunton, having met with financial reverses, was in a quandry and stated his position to Kelly, who said, "Jack, you know my range and my cattle; take my foreman with you, and select what you need. When you get paid for your beef, you can then pay me for my cattle." This was done. No written obligation was necessary. Hunton's word was sufficient. How many men are there of today who could enjoy the same trust as was reposed in Jack Hunton?

Another character was Butcher Phillips, a soldier at Fort Laramie, who acted as "post butcher" and who, on his discharge from the army, engaged in the stock business in a small way. He became very wealthy, owning a large number of cattle. Eventually he became a heavy beef contractor for these Government posts.

There was also a Portugese Philips, who had a wonderful history in that country, as it was he who carried the famous dispatch from Fort Phil Kearney to Fort Laramie in the year 1866, announcing to the world the great Phil Kearney massacre by the Sioux. This massacre was headed by the great Sioux chief, Red Cloud, and was somewhat similar to the Custer massacre. However, it was not as disastrous as far as numbers were concerned. there being about one hundred massacred.

Phil Kearney was a very isolated post, situated about two hundred miles northwest of Fort Laramie. One clear and very cold morning, when snow covered the ground to the depth of six inches, the Sioux by ruse inveigled about two-thirds of the soldiers stationed there to attack them. The Sioux retreating, this body of troops foolishly followed them into an ambush, where a large body of hidden Sioux attacked and completely annihilated them, not a man escaping.

This left the post with but few soldiers, but with quite a number of women, wives of the officers and soldiers. The Sioux, knowing these conditions, immediately surrounded the post and for two days and nights held a great war dance, flaunting the scalps of their victims where they could plainly be seen from the post. The commanding officer, realizing the great danger, knew that their only hope for rescue was in getting assistance from Fort Laramie. He therefore called for a volunteer to run their cordon of Indians with a dispatch.

Portugese Phillips, who was an ex-Hudson Bay hunter and who had lived for many years among the Sioux, having a squaw for a wife, and who at this time was the post interpreter, volunteered to make the attempt. Records show that at this time the thermometer registered thirty-two degrees below zero.

Phillips prepared to start off, selecting a white horse on account of its color being similar to the snow and not as easily distinguished as a dark one. He attached a sixty foot lariat to the horse, but knowing that horses often shook themselves, making considerable noise, if saddled, he did not use either saddle or bridle. In taking this precaution, he avoided attracting the attention of the Indians.

With a small supply of hard tack and dried meat in his pockets, Portugese Phillips left the post at midnight on his perilous journey. He crawled on his knees, leading his horse,—he being sixty feet in advance—and by daylight he had passed safely through the Indian lines. Then mounting his horse, he carried his dispatch to the commanding officer. His hands, knees, and feet were badly frozen, but he refused to remain at Fort Laramie and insisted on returning with the troops, stating that his squaw and children were among those in danger. He was put in an ambulance and placed in charge of two army physicians, who saved his limbs.

The command arrived at Fort Kearney just in the nick of time, as the Indians were gradually closing in on their victims—when seeing the large number of soldiers coming to the relief of the post, they retreated and the post was saved. Phillips, who proved himself a great hero, lies today in an unmarked grave somewhere in the vicinity of Fort Laramie, and I doubt very much whether even if a large reward were offered, a single man could point out his grave.

Another character at Fort Laramie during my time was an Irishman named Pat Brophy. Years before I knew him, he had crossed the Platte river to the north side and was sitting on the bank fishing, when five young Sioux bucks approached, one of them suddenly shooting him in the abdomen. Brophy retaining his senses, knew that his only chance lay in his feigning he was dead, which he did. Submitting to being scalped by two of the Indians and after they had disappeared, swimming across the river, he crawled out on the south side and lay by a log all that afternoon and night, and was found there more dead than alive, by two soldiers the following morning. The soldiers immediately conveyed him to the hospital, where he recovered from his wounds. The top of his head from where the scalp was removed, partially healed, but up to the time of his death was a running materated sore. The post physicians asserted that in all their professional experience, they had never known of anyone recovering from such an injury. Their opinion was that by his swimming the river and the cold water passing through the wound, this kept the wound clean and allayed the fever; also, that his lying in the open air all night was beneficial to the wound. Brophy lived in this condition for a number of years. Imagine, if possible, dear reader, the forethought and nerve displayed by this Irishman under these most trying circumstances; when a single move, or the batting of an eye, would have betrayed his wonderful cunning and caused his instant death.

I will now close my list of the few of the many old characters whom I knew at Fort Laramie, by describing one whom I considered the greatest of them all, from a military standpoint.

This was Ordinance-Sergeant Snyder. Snyder came to this post when it was established, having served in the Mexican War. He was eighty-six years of age when I first met him in 1873. He crossed the plains in an ox-wagon, the military using that mode of transportation in those days. Snyder in his own estimation, having been stationed there for so long a time, considered himself greater than the commanding officer, and was humored in this belief by the officers, soldiers and citizens.

He was a disciplinarian to an extreme and to incur his displeasure was very detrimental to one, as it was an unwritten law that Snyder was to be universally respected. He was wounded in his left thigh during the Mexican war, which caused him to have a pronounced limp when walking. He always displayed six medals on his left breast. These had been presented to him by the Government at various times as rewards for deeds of valor, and he was decidedly proud of them. When meeting Snyder, citizens as well as soldiers were expected to salute him in regular military style. When officers approached him, Snyder invariably stood at attention and saluted, and woe be to the officers who did not return the salute, for he would immediately remind them of their military training and would always conclude his rebuff with two loud coughs.

In addition to his duties as an Ordinance-Sergeant, Snyder was the garrison postmaster, which he considered a very responsible position. All citizens and soldiers were compelled to go in person for their mail to a small room set aside as a post office, and unless they saluted on approaching the window, he would motion them aside, telling them to go and discipline themselves. This compelled them to take their places at the end of the line and again await their turn. The officers' mail was delivered by him in person, and was carried in a leather bag—which hung by his side, showing the inscription "Officers' U. S. Mail, Sergeant Snyder, Postmaster." His first call was to the commanding officers' quarters, and then in succession, according to the officer's rank, ending with the 2nd-Lieutenant. Should any officer of lesser rank than those already called on, being ignorant of the Sergeant's custom, accost him and ask for his mail, the sergeant would salute and tell him that he would receive his mail at the proper time, in his turn. Army officers occasionally did this to try the old man, but the result was invariably the same.

In 1889, having grown very old, the Government concluded to send him to the National Soldiers' Home. Being informed of this, Snyder begged piteously to be allowed to remain at Fort Laramie and be buried there. The Government refused his request and ordered him to leave for Cheyenne and proceed from there by rail, to the Home. Poor Snyder obeyed, saying, "orders are orders, and I never disobeyed one in my life." But when they drove up with an ambulance drawn by four mules, the old man cried like a child and stated that he had "come to that post with an ox-team" and requested that he be allowed to depart in a like manner. His last request was granted and a six-ox team yoked to an old wagon was secured. Snyder and his belongings, which consisted of many relics of past days, were put into the wagon, preceded by the post band—the wagon surrounded by officers, according to their rank, and every soldier in the post marching in the rear. Thus, the old gentleman was escorted to the boundaries of the reservation, where the band played a final tune and the soldiers fired a farewell salute. A suitable escort continued with him to Cheyenne. After arriving at the Home, he lived but a few months. Thus ended the life of one of the greatest military characters of the early days at Fort Laramie.

One day during the summer of 1873, at about sundown, there rode into Fort Laramie, a young girl of about eleven years of age, astride a spotted Indian pony. She was enveloped in an Indian blanket, and for a time was thought to be an Indian squaw. In dismounting, she was discovered to be a white girl. A soldier took her to the commanding officer, but before he had had a chance to question her, she had fainted away from exhaustion. On being revived, she informed him that her name was Lizze Deering and that a party of Sioux Indians had killed her father and mother, some miles up the Platte river, and that a Sioux squaw had given her the pony and blanket and directed her to ride to the post.

The commanding officer immediately ordered a company of cavalry to find the spot, and also gave orders for an ambulance to be sent along to bring the bodies. I was commissioned to drive the ambulance. We started off that night and the next morning found the wagon minus the horses. In the wagon was an old man killed and scalped. With her hands tied to the rear wheels and her feet tied to stakes driven in the ground, we found a middle-aged woman. The Indians had abused her unspeakably, and in addition had removed the tongue bolt from the wagon, heated it red hot and forced it through the poor woman's abdomen, the same coming out above her left hip. The officer in charge made notes of the existing conditions, ordered the bodies removed to the ambulance, and trailing the wagon behind, we returned to Fort Laramie. The young girl in the meantime, had told the following story:

They had been traveling along the river bank, slowly; her father sitting in front driving the team, and she and her mother sitting back of him covered by the wagon sheet. Suddenly, a shot was heard

which killed her father. Immediately three young
buck Indians jumped up in the front of the wagon,
she and her mother quickly jumping out from the
rear. They were at once seized by three other Indians,
and tying the girl to a cottonwood tree and the mother
as previously described, they commenced their ill-
treatment of the elder woman and thus subjected the
young girl to witness the horrible torture of her
mother.

Suddenly, there appeared a young squaw, who
compelled the Indians to release her. The squaw
ordered the Indians away, and after taking the horses
and all articles of value, they left. Quieting the child,
the squaw gave her the pony and blanket and started
her for the post. This was the first known instance
of the kind that had ever occurred among the Sioux,
as the squaws were generally known to be more vicious
with a white person, and particularly with one of their
own sex.

No one in that country could understand the
squaw's reason for treating the young girl so kindly.
Later on, the commanding officer, on inquiry through
the post interpreter who was a squaw-man, learned
that this young Indian girl was the daughter of a
chief and that she had used her power to compel these
young bucks to release this girl, but no one knows to
this day what prompted her to do so. It is possible
that the post interpreter's squaw knew, but ·if she
did, she never made it known. Perhaps it was sisterly
instinct, or perhaps an act of the Supreme Being,
that made her deviate from the cruel Indian custom
and perform an act of mercy.

The Deering family were from Pike county, Missouri, and their destination was Oregon. This young
girl remained in Fort Laramie for some time, but was
finally located by her uncle, who took her back to
Missouri.

During the conversation with Tom Hunton some years ago, I alluded to this massacre. He told me that on the very spot where that wagon stood, a stone monument had been erected by the women of Wyoming, with an appropriate inscription of the details of the massacre. In addition to this, they also presented to the Chief's daughter, who is now an old woman, living at Pine Ridge Agency, a medal made from gold mined in Wyoming. On one side of the medal is an engraving of the wagon and on the reverse side, suitable words of explanation. Tom also informed me that she valued the medal very highly and wears it continually.

In 1867, prior to my time in Wyoming, the Government issued to the troops at Fort Phil Kearney, a breech-loading gun, called the Spencer carbine, the first of the kind used in that particular part of the country. They being out of wood at the post, the commanding officer detailed twenty-five six-mule teams to haul a fresh supply. The wood was at a point twenty miles distant from the post. He also furnished an escort of fifty infantry soldiers, as the Sioux were very dangerous, having the year previously committed a massacre at that post. The Indians knew nothing of these repeating guns, and the officer in charge of the escort was well aware of this fact.

The teams had not proceeded far on their mission when they were attacked by a large body of Sioux. The officer corraled the teams and instructed the men not to fire until they could see the white of the Indians' eyes and when he gave the order to fire, to pump it in fast. The Indians were in the habit of forcing fire, and then charging, thinking the troops were armed with the old muzzle-loading guns. Finally the officer gave the command to fire. After the first volley, the Indians charged in a body; and such a surprise they received, resulting in some eighty being killed, which taught them a lesson for future consideration. Prior to making this attack, they had stationed their squaws and families on a high hill, expecting to witness another Phil Kearney massacre; but after receiving this warm reception, they and their squaws made a very hasty retreat—less in number, but wiser in experience. And for many years these Indians had a great horror of the "foot soldiers"—as they termed the infantry.

CHAPTER XI.

GREAT POWER INVESTED IN COMMANDING OFFICERS
OF THE FRONTIER POSTS—LIEUTENANT ROBINSON
KILLED BY INDIANS—A NUT FOR SCIENTISTS TO
CRACK—THE BARREN SPOT ON THE PRAIRIE—
AMUSING INCIDENTS.

I WISH to give the reader an idea of the power assumed by the commanding officers of the various frontier posts, and would ask the reader that he kindly bear in mind that these posts were situated a long way from civilization.

The commanding officers had the power to do anything they chose to either a soldier or a citizen. The latter they seemed to dislike very much, and in many cases were very severe with them. Many, like myself, following the occupation of a government teamster, were compelled to take any insults the officers would thrust upon them, knowing well that if they offended the officer, he would drive them from the post and, what was then termed, "blackball" them, and in order to get another position, the teamster would have to go to some other post and change his name. I have met in my life a few old government teamsters, who had changed their names so often that if one should call them by their real name, they would hesitate before responding, as they had almost forgotten it.

In my time at Fort Laramie the commanding officer was General Smith. He was a very severe man and greatly disliked by both soldier and citizen. He was quite old at the time I knew him, with gray hair, and a large military mustache, and a goatee. This gave him a fierce look. He always wore a military cloak, which was lined with a bright red material and the corner of this he would throw over his left shoulder, exposing the lining, and with his gold handled sword at his side, in his estimation he was lord of all he surveyed. The soldiers used to say that if by mistake he looked kindly at one of them, he would go to his quarters and have his orderly tie him to a post and horsewhip him. This was what the soldiers called "doing penance."

One day I was leading three mules with halters on; attached to them were chain halters shanks. I was taking the mules to the blacksmith's shop to be shod. A government mule is very hard to lead, especially away from the corral, and I was having a difficult time with them. Suddenly a soldier said to me, "General Smith wants to see you." I asked him where. He motioned his head toward the parade grounds—there stood General Smith. The soldier was his orderly. I tied the mules to a nearby post and walked up to "His Majesty." He asked me where I was going with those mules. I told him to the blacksmith's shop. He grunted, turned his head and walked away. He never knew what passed through my mind. I returned to my mules and completed my journey.

The gala day in these isolated posts once a month, was "dress parade." All soldiers turned out, including the band. They arranged seats on the edge of the parade grounds for the officers' wives and visiting friends. Citizens employees also attended, but they were supposed to take up their position on the opposite side of the parade ground. The soldiers marched around, the band played martial airs, led by "His Majesty" the General. When this was over, the officers and their wives, and visiting friends, would parade arm in arm, praising and criticising.

I had a teamster friend whom I bunked with while at the post, our sleeping quarters being enclosed by a corral, on the opposite side from where the mules were stabled. This boy's name was Charley O'Brien. He was a very wild young fellow and absolutely fearless. We had had a pay day about this time, and he and I went up the river one afternoon to a ranch where they sold whiskey and where they also had three or four girls with whom we could dance. There were many of these ranches in the vicinity of the post and they were called "Hog Ranches." Why so called, I could not say, as I never saw any hogs around them, but think that perhaps it had reference to the girls as they were a very low, tough set.

We stayed there that night until about ten o'clock, returning to the post pretty well filled up with "bug juice," commonly called whiskey. In crossing the corral, O'Brien remarked:

"Tomorrow is dress parade!"

General Smith had a very fine horse which he rode at these parades. To take care of this horse, he had a soldier detailed and whom the soldiers termed "dog robber." All officers had soldier servants and they were all known by the same name. Why this was given them, I am unable to state. However, O'Brien suggested that we go to the stable in the corner of the corrall where this horse was and together shave his tail. At first I refused, but O'Brien explained to my satisfaction that General Smith would blame the "dog-robber" or some other soldier, and never would suspect a citizen. I finally agreed, and getting a candle and shears, we started off to the stable, I holding the candle while O'Brien clipped the hair from the horse's tail. The poor horse, not having had this kind of treatment before, could not understand it. He would turn his head around, looking first at one and then the other, and I really felt sorry for him. However, we finished the job and lo, and behold! such a change in a horse, you can't imagine. His tail, while larger than a rat's, looked very similar to one. We gathered up the hair the best we could, hiding it in a pile of manure. We then went to our bunk.

Teamsters were compelled to rise early in the morning. But O'Brien and I, not feeling very well, remained in bed longer than the balance. We were finally awakened by a loud noise in the corral. Dressing ourselves hurriedly, we went out to the corral. There we found the "dog robber" with all the teamsters standing around him. He was waving his hands in the air and moaning like a man in great pain.

"My God," he was saying, "the General will kill me when hears of this."

O'Brien, stepping up to him said: "My good man, go at once and report this before the soldier escapes who committed this dastardly act."

But the poor fellow was afraid to do so. O'Brien then told him he would go up with him. This quieted him, and together they went to General Smith's quarters, O'Brien making the report. The General immediately came down to the corral, looked at the horse, and turning around to O'Brien, said: "My man, I will give you five hundred dollars if you will find the soldier or soldiers who committed this act."

O'Brien bowed respectfully and told the General he would try his best to earn the reward. The expression on the General's face was a sight never to be forgotten. His face was naturally red, but in his great anger it turned a bluish cast. He coughed a few times and throwing his head erect, strutted back to his quarters, the maddest man in Fort Laramie. There was no dress parade that day. About an hour after General Smith had left, the horse was taken away,—to where I cannot say, for no one ever saw him again at Fort Laramie in my time.

In 1892 I was employed to manage a transfer company in Tacoma, Washington. After taking charge

and in looking over the books, we found a great many
old unpaid bills. I suggested to the president of the
company, "Woody Sprague," that we employ a young
man who had the ability to collect these old bills, also
suggesting that we pay him a liberal commission. He
agreed with me and we inserted an advertisement in
the daily paper. Six persons answered the advertisement. The matter being in my hands, I interviewed
these applicants, and finally selected a young man
whom, in my judgment, I thought the best fitted for
the position. His name was L. Smith.

After Smith had been working there for about
two weeks, he happened to hear me mention "Fort
Laramie," and asked me if I had ever lived there. I
told him yes, and that I used to drive a six-mule team
at that post. He then informed me that he was born
there.

"Why!" I said, "you are the son of General Smith
then, aren't you?"

He replied, "Yes, did you know my father?"

I told him I did and asked him where his father
was, and if alive.

"Why, yes," he answered. "He is living here on the
retired list."

He also said that when he went home that night
he would tell his father, adding, that if his father felt
well enough, he would bring him down to see me.

I made no reply to this, well knowing that if the
General was as he used to be, he would not come; but
to my great surprise, the following afternoon at about
three o'clock in walked the young man with his father.

The General still wore his military cloak with one
side thrown over his shoulder, and did not look a day
older than he did at Fort Laramie. The young man
introduced us. The General did not shake hands or

bow, but said: "My son informs me that you were at Fort Laramie during the time I was in command there?"

"I replied, "Yes, sir."

He coughed once or twice, saying: "I am always pleased to meet anyone who has lived at Fort Laramie." Looking around, he then remarked, "This is quite a concern!" referring to the transfer business. Without further comment, he left the office, his son accompanying him. This ended our meeting.

The following morning I asked his son what his father thought of the "ex-mule-skinner," and if in his lifetime he had ever heard his father speak of the "tail-shaving" incident. He looked at me for a moment and then said, "No; but I have heard my mother mention it, but she has warned us never to discuss the matter in father's presence, which we never do."

He then went on: "If you will not be offended I will answer your questions regarding what my father thinks of you."

I assured him I would not.

He then told me that his father had said, "That fellow looks all right; but I never knew him at Fort Laramie, as I always detested teamsters," and advised him not to become too familiar with me, as his past experience had taught him that teamsters were a d— bad set.

I then told him to tell his mother, and through her his father, that if that five hundred dollar reward still stood good, I was sure I could produce one of the men who helped shave the horse's tail.

The boy laughed and said, "I would not approach father on the subject again if you were to present me with a thousand dollars, as it would greatly annoy my mother, and am sure it would hasten my father's death," and I judged from his remark that it was a forbidden subject in their family. The young man continued in our employ until I quit the transfer company. His father, I heard, died four years later.

In the year 1870 the Government installed a portable sawmill at a point named Harney's Peak, forty miles north of Fort Laramie, their intention being to manufacture lumber to be used at the Fort. The Indians became very troublesome, however, and the Government was forced to remove the machinery to Fort Laramie and there erect the sawmill. In the early spring of 1873 they detailed twenty-five teams to transport some of the logs, I being one of the teamsters. We had an infantry escort commanded by Lieutenant Robinson. On returning from this trip, Robinson took with him his first sergeant and his orderly. All three were mounted. Leaving the teams early in the morning, he told the wagonmaster that he would meet us in camp about four o'clock in the afternoon and that he would ride across country and kill a deer, the second lieutenant being left in charge of the escort.

We made camp about four o'clock and were about to unharness the mules, when the orderly suddenly appeared on foot and informed us that Lieutenant Robinson and the sergeant had been killed by the Indians. He very much exaggerated his story by excitedly saying that half of the Sioux nation were on the war path. The lieutenant in command ordered the boys to unload the logs, and if one ever wanted to see soldiers work, they could surely have seen them then. These logs that would ordinarily have taken a full hour to unload were off the wagons in five minutes. Soldiers climbing on the running gears of the wagons, we started for the post. The mules seemed to scent the danger, and in a few minutes were on a wild run. All was excitement.

I looked back once or twice from my saddle mule and it was surely a laughable sight to see those soldiers bouncing like rubber balls and hanging on for dear life. Many of them dropped their guns, being unable to hold on to the wagon and their guns as well. What we most wanted was to get to the post, where we arrived at midnight.

I don't know what the lieutenant reported to the commanding officer, but I do know that I was routed out of my blankets by the wagonmaster about four A. M. and told to hitch up four mules to an ambulance and report to the commanding officer, where I found two companies of cavalry ready to start in search of the bodies. Taking the still frightened orderly along, we left on the gallop, finding the bodies about eight o'clock in the morning on the bank of a stream, both killed and scalped. On being more closely questioned, the orderly admitted that there were but five Indians in the party, whom we presumed were merely hunting. He also stated that Lieutenant Robinson, on seeing the Indians approach, ran off, the sergeant following. The orderly dismounting, secreted himself in the rocks and was not molested, the Indians merely taking his horse, but they followed Robinson and the sergeant, killing both of them.

In the year 1869, prior to my time, the telegraph line between Fort Fetterman and Laramie became grounded. They dispatched from Fort Fetterman a sergeant and four soldiers with a six-mule team to repair this line. They discovered about four miles from the post that the wire had broken loose from the top of the telegraph pole. This pole was situated at the head of a little canyon or wash-out. The sergeant ordered a soldier to carry the wire up and attach it, the three other men staying in the wagon with the team. While this man was up the pole, five young Sioux Indians crawled up this canyon, shooting and killing him. The team became frightened, running back to Fort Fetterman, leaving the sergeant alone. He, seeing the Indians, also ran toward the post. When he got about twenty steps on the north side of the wagon road, the Indians shot him. They then scalped and mutilated the body horribly, and it is said, cut out his heart, and also cut his ears and nose off. The team in the meantime having arrived at the post, they immediately sent soldiers out to look for the sergeant and private. Finding the sergeant as stated, and after removing him, they drove a large stake where his head lay, putting on this stake an old buffalo skull.

When I went into that country, I heard the story many times that where that body lay, grass had never grown after the killing, while all around it was the very finest of grass. This spot was situated on the top of what was called La Bonte Hill. The first time I went to Fetterman, several other teamsters and myself examined this spot; in fact, all teams or horsemen going by and knowing of this phenomenon, always examined it. I have seen it myself twenty times and am satisfied in my mind that this spot at one time was a deserted ant hill, which the elements had flattened down.

While in Cheyenne, Wyoming, in 1912, I met a great many old-timers, and in talking with them I mentioned the incident. They all remembered it well. One of them, Bob Carson, said he had visited the spot two weeks prior to this time and that it was still barren. Old-timers believed that this grass was killed by the blood of the sergeant. I remarked that I thought it was an old ant hill. They looked at me a little while, one of them saying: "Young, since you have been living in large cities and meeting these d— fool scientists, they have talked that into your head.

We have had four or five of them tell us the same thing," and to a man they stuck to the theory that the blood had killed the grass. A year ago my old friend, Hi Kelley, while visiting his son in Portland, took dinner at my house. I happened to mention this subject to him and he immediately said, "Yes, that place is barren yet; made so by the blood of the poor sergeant."

While at Fort Laramie many amusing incidents happened; incidents which were so ludicrous as to upset the dignity of the company commanders, and on various occasions that of the commanding officer.

I recall three such incidents. A recruit was sent out to Laramie and for some days he got along very well, but when one of the old-timers called his attention to the fact that he had been eating with the mess for some days without butter checks, he asked where they were obtained. A soldier named Mickey Flinn informed him that the captain always issued such as were needed. The recruit immediately set out in search of the captain. His blouse was unbuttoned and his round-topped army cap sat at an angle of 40 degrees on his head. Knocking on the door, the captain, who was known as a strict disciplinarian, appeared.

"Say, cap," said the recruit, "by heck, I have got to have some of them butter checks."

"Some what?" exploded the captain.

"Butter checks, I gad, butter checks, 'cause them d— fools down at the cook house won't let me eat any more until I get 'em."

The captain looked at the man and grabbing his cap from his head, started for the company quarters, where he met the first sergeant of the company, asking him who sent this man to his quarters dressed in such an unmilitary costume, demanding butter checks. "What does it mean?"

The recruit spoke up, saying, "The sergeant is not the man who sent me."

The captain then asked him if he could point out the man who did. He replied, "Yes."

They then formed the company in line, and walking down looking at first one and then the other, pointed out Flinn as the man, who denied the charge, and calling on the other men who substantiated the denial. The captain could retain himself no longer, and throwing the recruit's cap on the floor, burst out in a roar of laughter, and walking from the quarters, turned around at the door, and in a loud voice ordered the sergeant to give the man some butter checks.

Between the parade ground and the Platte River were situated three very large stacks of hay, which were quite a distance from the guard house. Around those stacks of hay night and day was stationed a guard, whose duty it was to walk around them. It came a recruit's time to take this post. His hours were from ten o'clock at night until two o'clock in the morning. This was considered a very lonely post. About fifty yards below the stacks was an old Indian burying ground. The older soldiers confidentially told this recruit that at the hour of twelve, midnight, the spirits of these departed Indians often appeared. They warned him not to shoot at these spirits as it was useless, but if any did appear, to shoot his gun in the air and they would come to his relief. The day previous they had taken a soldier to the hospital who had an ulcerated tooth, the pain of which made him delirious. About midnight he walked out of the hospital with a bed sheet thrown over his head and shoulders. He wandered down by the hay stacks toward the Platte River. This recruit, seeing him in that garb, knew at once that he was one of the Indian spirits, and as directed, shot his gun in the air, when the corporal of the guard and two soldiers went to his assistance. By the time they arrived there, the supposed spirit had disappeared. They then told the recruit that he was nervous and imagined he saw this spirit. However, he insisted strongly that he was sure he had seen one and refused to stand guard any longer. They finally compelled him to do so.

The next morning the post surgeon in going through the hospital, discovered that the soldier with the ulcerated tooth was missing, and hearing of the incident related, instructed that search be made for him. They found him lying on his stomach on the river bank with his head in the water, dead—presumably drowned.

Another recruit, hearing his companions talking about post guard and not knowing what it meant, asked the corporal what one did on post guard. The corporal replied, "Don't show your ignorance before the soldiers, as they will josh you. Go get your gun and come with me and I will instruct you."

They walked out to the rear of the quarters, the corporal picking up a large wagon spoke and an axe, with which he drove the spoke in the ground, leaving an exposure of about a foot. He then instructed the recruit to hold his gun with both hands and balance himself by standing on this stake with one foot, and when he got so that he could do so, he would be prepared to stand post guard. The corporal then informed the rest of the company what he had done and through the windows they watched this fellow for a half hour, trying to balance himself on the stake. Finally he gave it up, marching into the quarters, when, of course, they all laughed at him.

CHAPTER XII.

THE SLEEP OF THE JUST—IN THE PLATTE RIVER—
GOVERNMENT'S CIVILIZING OF THE SIOUX—LIGHT
ON INDIAN POLICIES—ORIGIN OF THE SIOUX IN-
DIAN FUED—A DRUNKEN OFFICER AND A THIRTY-
DOLLAR COW — AN AGENCY EMPLOYEE — THE
WHITE MAN WITH THE REMARKABLE EYE—QUEER
EXPERIENCES WITH THE SIOUX—SOME OF THE
FAMOUS CHIEFS.

IN November, 1873, there arrived at Fort Laramie two teams from Red Cloud Agency, driven by Pat Simmons and Mike Dunn. They informed me that I could now get a position on the Agency and that they were on their way to Cheyenne for supplies, and would return in seven days, and instructed me to meet them on the south side of the Platte River, at the lower crossing, twenty-five miles east of Fort Laramie, as they would camp there that night. As per this agreement I left Fort Laramie on the morning of the seventh day and walked the entire distance, alone. The Platte River is a very treacherous stream and full of quicksand, but at certain places it can be crossed, owing to a gravel bottom. These places were called fords, the location of which it was necessary for one to know in crossing the stream, to avoid getting into the quicksands. Should one, in crossing unfortunately miss the ford, there would be great danger in losing his team and wagon. I have known instances where they had gotten into the quicksand, barely escaping with their own lives or the lives of their teams, as it was utterly impossible to get the wagons out. In one case, a wagon entirely disappeared in forty-eight hours.

On my journey to this crossing, owing to the sandy road, I walked very slowly, and darkness overtook me before my arrival. Becoming bewildered, I strayed out into the sand hills and came to the realization that I was lost, but knowing that the Platte River lay in a northerly direction, I started that way and finally found it about midnight. Tired and cold and being without blankets, I tried to find some driftwood with which to make a fire, but the night being so dark, I was unsuccessful. I then walked back from the river to keep warm and stumbled onto an old cock of hay which had been left by Government contractors, they having left it there while cutting wild hay. I lifted it up and crawled under it. In time my shelter became warm, and hungry and footsore, I fell asleep. However, before doing so, I heard a noise that struck me with terror,—the howling of wolves!

My feelings can better be imagined than described, and it was only from sheer exhaustion that I fell asleep. When I awoke, the sun was well up in the heavens. The teams had crossed the river and I found that I was two miles above the ford. I took my clothes off, tied them in a bundle on my head and waded into that cold Platte River. I got along all right until near the north side, when I unfortunately got off the ford and into the quicksand. I now found my progress exceedingly slow and difficult. When I tried to step ahead, my foot would be fast in the sand, and it was only by continually plunging that I was able to reach the shore in a very exhausted condition. I dressed and went to a ranch kept by a squaw-man named "Nick Jannesse." I asked him if he had seen the Agency teams. He said yes, that they had broken camp four hours ago. He gave me breakfast and I started after them, catching up with them about noon in the sand hills. The boys were very glad to see me, but not more so than I was to see them. They had thought I was not coming. We arrived at the Agency in due time and I reported to Dr. Seville, who took me into his office to give me instructions as one of his employees.

To have the reader understand the situation as it existed in the summer of 1873, I will explain on what plan they proposed to civilize the Sioux.

The Indians at that time were in the hands of the Interior Department of the Government, their intention being to civilize them through kindness, the military having nothing whatever to do with them. At this time the Sioux domain comprised all lands from the British Northwest as far south as Wyoming and east to Nebraska. The Platte River was the dividing line. Fort Laramie was the nearest post to the Agency.

Before giving my experiences while on Red Cloud Agency, I wish to take the reader back some years before my time. I think in the fifties or early sixties, a certain officer in Fort Laramie owned a cow worth thirty dollars. This cow by some means strayed across the Platte River, where there was a large camp of Sioux Indians. One of the Indians killed this cow. The officer who owned it, took a few soldies over to the Indian camp and demanded from the chief the Indian who killed the cow. This officer was drunk at the time. His demand was met with refusal, whereupon he shot the chief, killing him. Prior to this time the Indians were friendly with the whites. They would steal their horses but were not in open war, as was the case after this occurrence. I cannot recall this officer's name or the name of the chief killed, but doubtless their names as well as the circumstances can be found on record in the War Department at Washington.

A few days after this incident a company of soldiers were on the south side of the Platte, about twenty-five miles below Fort Laramie. They were not aware of the trouble on account of the cow. The Indians, about one thousand in number, attacked and killed the entire company, numbering sixty. They were all buried in the same grave near where they fell, with the exception of the lieutenant in command, who was taken to Fort Laramie. After this it was war to the death between Sioux and white man. It was all caused by a drunken officer and an old thirty-dollar cow; and many whites have lost their lives since then through this occurrence.

I will now return to the Agency. Dr. Seville, the agent, of whom I have before made mention, came from Sioux City, Iowa. He was a fine man and I understand he left a large practice in Sioux City to take this position. His salary was not large but there were many ways for him to make money independent of his salary. Dr. Seville explained to me how I should act. First, I was not to carry any firearms. I was not to resent any insults from an Indian, no matter what he said or did to me; I was to treat them kindly, etc.

"Now," said Seville, "if you are sure you can live up to those rules, you may go to work. Your wages will be one hundred dollars per month and found."

I accepted his terms and became an employe of the Agency. There were twenty-one of us employed there, Otis Johnson being chief clerk. Others whom I recall were Mart Gibbons, who was corral boss; Ben Tibbetts, agency butcher; Paddy Simmons, Mike Dunne and Dutch Joe, teamsters. Tom Monahan was boss carpenter; Mr. Appleton was agency farmer, and we also had there a negro named "Alec," who later put on a breech-clout and became a full-fledged Sioux warrior. I often wonder what ever became of this negro. He is worthy of mention. He was about twenty-five years of age, perfectly built and very intelligent. He spoke the Sioux language fluently and was a great favorite with the tribe. He gradually adopted their ways from preference, it evidently being the height of his ambition to become one of them.

The first day I worked I was carrying a board on my shoulder, when a young buck caught it by the end, and swinging it around, knocked me down. I jumped up and ran at him, mad as a March hare. Some one yelled at me, "Look out, Young! You will lose your job if you hit him." I remembered my instructions from the agent and stopped.

These Sioux were very mischievous and were continually playing tricks on us boys. We also had on the Agency a character named Molasses Bill, this name being given him on account of his love for molasses. He was employed as a carpenter and had one glass eye. One day Bill and I were on the roof of the commissary putting on tar paper. The wind was blowing hard as it often did, and the air was full of fine sand, which got into Bill's eye, causing him much annoyance. This compelled him to remove the glass eye and wipe it off with his handkerchief. An Indian named Grass saw the act and was much surprised to know that we had a white man who could remove his eye at will. Grass motioned him down from the building and with other Indians made him remove the eye again. In doing so, the Indians all set up a great howl and thought Bill the wonder of the age, and Bill for the next few days was kept busy taking out and putting in that glass eye. After some days it seemed to affect his head and he became insane. The agent was finally compelled to furnish him with an Indian escort and send him to Fort Laramie.

I will here mention a few names of the chiefs and more prominent Indians, but before doing so will explain how Indians derive their names.

The Indians do not christen their children but select names from some act which has attracted an older Indian while the one named is in his infancy. For instance, take the name "Man Afraid of His Horses." This particular name was given him when a child by some older Indian having seen him afraid of horses. As he grew into manhood, he was called "Man Afraid of His Horses," and while I lived on the Agency this Indian had a grown son, and to distinguish him from his father, he was called "Young Man Afraid of His Horses." There was no exception to this rule and there is no doubt that their names were derived in this way.

"Red Cloud" was the acknowledged chief of the Agency and the most powerful. Their power originated from two causes. "Red Cloud" was a great warrior in his early days; while other Indians, for instance, "Little Wound," got his great power from the number of his relatives. They were divided into bands. There was "Red Cloud's" band, "Little Wound's" band, "Man Afraid of His Horses'" band, etc. Then again, they had great diplomats. One was "Spotted Tail." He would be ranked in the same order as our great James G. Blaine or Roscoe Conkling, and all treaties formed with other tribes or with the United States Government, were submitted to him before being ratified, and it was from this trait of character that he was all-powerful.

Referring to "Little Wound" reminds me of the night mentioned when I made my tenderfoot trip with my Indian companion. The reason for my companion's excitement was that "Little Wound's" band of braves had been on a hunting expedition in the eastern part of Wyoming, where they ran across a camp of old men and women of the Pawnee tribe. The young Pawnee bucks being out on the hunt and having left the old men and women in camp, this "Little Wound's" band killed them all, amounting to about one hundred, and these young bucks were returning to the Agency the night we met them on the road; they had heard from their scouts that the Pawnee Indians were about to attack the Sioux in retaliation for killing their old men and women. I afterward saw them in their war dance with those poor old folks' scalps. This I will explain later.

Another powerful and notorious Indian was "Sword," who was a very bad one whom we much feared. He had been wounded in the groin by a white man some years before, which made him hate the white race, and knowing his hatred for the white man, we always kept at a safe distance until we knew he had left the Agency. He afterward died from the wound. Another very prominent Indian, "American Horse," and who was very friendly to the whites, had a national reputation, having visited the Great Father at Washington in company with other Sioux chiefs, and where he had promised the Government that he would use his great influence and his best endeavors to keep the Indians from killing the whites, stealing their horses, and committing other depredations, which he did to the best of his ability. I will speak of him later and show how he kept his word.

Another Indian character was "Chief Grass" of whom I have spoken proviously. Grass could speak English fairly well and he had a very comprehensive brain. For instance, we built a sawmill nine miles from the Agency with which we cut the lumber to construct the buildings. Grass one day, with some other Indians, wanted to see this mill in operation. The boss sawyer of the mill was named Charley. Charley was quite a loafer and did not keep the mill in operation half of the time. I was delegated by the agent to go out to this sawmill with these Indians. When we arrived there, the mill was not in operation. Grass turned around to me and remarked:

"What's the matter? Mill no run."

I replied, "Ask Charley; he's boss man here."

Grass did so.

Charley replied, "I have to gum the saw."

Grass looked at him a while and said, "Me think you no good. Too much loaf all the time. Dam big expense on us Indians."

Then turning to me, he said: "You good man. You start mill up."

I had a hard time explaining to Grass that I knew nothing about running a sawmill. They then looked the mill over and we returned to the Agency. Grass called on the agent and entered a strong complaint against Charley. After counselling some time, the agent finally promised that he would see that the mill was kept running in future, and this seemed to satisfy old Grass.

Another prominent and very bad Indian was "Red Dog." He always wore a hunting jacket made entirely of scalps that he himself had taken during his lifetime. In the back of this jacket was a woman's scalp. She in life was a white woman and a blonde. I suppose he killed and scalped her in the Minnesota massacre years prior to this time, as he took a very active part in that affair. I could have purchased that jacket at one time for about five dollars worth of powder and lead, and wished in later days that I had done so, as today it would be worth a large sum of money.

CHAPTER XIII.

MORE NOTED SIOUX CHARACTERS—SITTING BULL'S
RIGHT BOWER IN THE CUSTER MASSACRE—BEN
TIBBETT'S GOOD ADVICE—INDIANS AS BEGGARS
AND DRINKERS—RED CLOUD'S BOY—SAVED FROM
RED CLOUD'S "BAD HEART"—A HIGH-GRADE IN-
DIAN FUNERAL—RED CLOUD AND HIS FINAL
HAND-WASHING.

IN the preceding chapter I mentioned a number of
prominent as well as bad Sioux. I next recall Big
Foot, who took a big part in the Custer massacre.
He was Sitting Bull's right-hand bower in that
affair. There were also many lesser lights called
Indian soldiers.

The most popular white man on the Agency was
Ben Tibbetts. He was employed as agency butcher.
His duty was to take care of the old, discarded
squaws and men. He had lived among the Indians
for a great many years and knew a great many of
them; spoke their language, knew their habits and had
an Indian squaw for a wife. This man took a great
interest in me and gave me some good advice regard
ing the Sioux. He told me never to give them anything, and that they were awful beggars. For instance, if one gave a Sioux fifty cents, the next day
he would want a dollar, and if refused, he became an
enemy. I took Ben's advice, only varying from it on
one occasion.

There was an old Indian named Gray Eyes, who
spoke English quite well, and one day he told me his
papoose was awful sick and that if he could secure
some red apples he had seen at the trading store, he
knew that they would make him well. These apples
would cost twenty-five cents. Instead of buying the

apples for him, as I should have done, I foolishly gave him the money. This he proceeded to invest in a bottle of Perry Davis' Painkiller. The next day his squaw came and told the agent that one of the white men had given her Indian some poison water that had almost killed him. She was referring to the pain-killer, which he had drunk and which made him very sick. The following day Gray Eyes again appeared and told me what an immense amount of good the red apples had done his papoose. He wanted fifty cents more, so that he could get a larger supply and completely cure the little one. This I refused, and it re-sulted in my being called all manner of names and losing the friendship of Gray Eyes, verifying what Tibbetts had told me.

There were two trading stores on the Agency. One was kept by Mr. Deere and the other by Yates & Reshaw. Both stores carried a full supply of Jamaica ginger, Perry Davis' Painkiller and cheap bay rum, and the Indians bought large quantities of each. It was their custom to adulterate this and drink it in place of whiskey. They would take the bay rum, pour it into a cup of water and, after skimming the oil for the sur-face, they would dring it. This often resulted in their getting beastly drunk and finally the agent was forced to prohibit the sale of the stuff at the stores. Bad white men would bring whiskey, of the vilest kind, on the Agency and trade it to the Indians for Buffalo robes, blankets and horses. While under the influence of this vile stuff, they became very quarrelsome and dangerous to us white men employed there.

Chief Red Cloud had a favorite son about eighteen years of age, whom he expected in time to succeed him. Indians show a great affection for their sons, much more so than for their daughters. No matter how bad the boys became, they were never punished, but were more appreciated. Red Cloud was completely wrapped

up in his son and had predicted a great future for him.
The son became severely ill, which had a very depressing effect on Red Cloud. One day Tom Monahan and
I were at work on the stable roof, when suddenly we
heard a great deal of shooting. Looking down at Red
Cloud's camp, which was close by, we saw the Indians
in a state of great excitement, firing off their guns and
six-shooters. I remarked to Tom that Red Cloud's boy
must be dead or dying, and that we had better lose
no time in getting into safer quarters.

The shooting referred to was the last act of the
Indians before the death of one of their number, as it
was supposed to drive away the evil spirits. Quickly
sliding off the roof, Tom and I started through a hole
in the stockade fence to go across to our quarters. The
Agency quarters not being finished, we were compelled
to eat and sleep in two houses made of slabs about
fifty yards from the stockade. As we emerged we
suddenly met Red Cloud, who was naked, with the exception of his breechclout and moccasins. With a knife
he had slashed his breast, arms and thighs, causing
blood to run freely down his body. He certainly presented a ghastly appearance. This slashing was an in-
dication of great grief and Red Cloud, with his head
bowed down, gun in hand and crying bitterly, was
indeed a pitiful object.

Indians hearts, as they termed them, became bad
through the losing of a very dear friend or relative.
When in that condition, they had the idea that they
must kill a white man to atone for their loss and make
their hearts "good again." Monahan and I lost no
time getting back through that opening and fortunately
were not seen by Red Cloud. He entered the gate of the
stockade and was met by Joe Bisnett, a half-breed, who
was the chief interpreter. Joe talked with him for
some time, telling him how sorry everyone was for
him, and added that as a great chief he should set a

good example for his tribe, and not attempt the injury
of a white man; that they were all his friends, sent
there by the great father at Washington for their good
and comfort. Joe finally brought his talk to a close by
suggesting to him that he accept a blanket as a peace
offering, but Red Cloud slowly shook his head and refused. As a last resort, Joe left him and, going to
the commissary, shortly returned with a bright red
blanket, urging Red Cloud to accept it. This had the
desired effect, and he finally nodded his head, indicating
that Joe had carried his point. Then the agent came
and sympathized with Red Cloud and told him what
good judgment he had used and how it would please
the great father at Washington. Red Cloud then returned to his lodge, where the body lay. Immediately,
the old squaws commenced their death cry, walking
around by the hundreds in a large circle, and giving
vent to their feelings. It was solemn and mournful in
the extreme, and no description could do it full justice.

The following day the agent sent word to Red Cloud
by Joe that he would like to talk with him at the office.
Red Cloud went and was requested to bury his son in
a box, something hitherto unknown among the Sioux.
It was urged that this new mode of burial would have
a very good effect on his tribe, and that it was in ac-
cordance with the custom of the white man. At first
Red Cloud refused. It seemed hard for him to give
up the old custom of wrapping the dead in skins and
burying them by lashing them to poles, which were laid
across the high limbs of trees. Finally, it being argued
that the new mode was another step of the Indians
toward civilization, Red Cloud consented. That night
the carpenter made the box and the scaffold, which we
hauled out the following morning to a high point about
a mile from the Agency. The agent then notified Red
Cloud all was ready.

The funeral started, consisting of all the Indians,
male and female, children and dogs, and was a sight

never to be forgotten. The body was wrapped tightly in blankets and hauled on a litter to its last resting place. Four other white men and myself put the body in the box, the Indians placing therein a gun, a liberal supply of ammunition, six pairs of moccasins, a spear, bow and arrows andtwo extra breechclouts, some eagles claws and beads. These, in the Sioux belief, were for his use in the happy hunting ground. Twenty head of ponies were then driven up and the shooting of them began. These were also for the use of the departed. The increased excitment caused by the shooting, bullets and arrows flew in all directions, made us very uneasy. Screwing the lid down tightly and raising the box on the scaffold, Monahan remarked, "Drive for the Agency as fast as you can." So I whipped up the mules and made faster time than had ever been made before, the occupants of the wagon, bouncing around like rubber balls.

Driving into the stockade, we closed the gates and for two hours listened in terror to the Sioux shooting and crying as though bedlam had let loose. The agent was very much alarmed and we all thought our last day had come. Gradually the uproar subsided and normal conditions prevailed once more. Some idea of the size of the funeral procession may be formed from the fact that there were fully five thousand in attendance. That evening about dark, we again heard the mournful cry of the squaws. Looking out, we saw large numbers of them walking in single file. They had provisions with them, carried in large receptacles, which they were taking to deposit at the foot of the scaffold. This performance was kept up for ten days. Each morning the provisions were gone, having been eaten by wolves. These provisions were supposed to last the dead 'till he should reach the rendezvous of the buffalo, after which they would not be needed.

The morning after the funeral, Red Cloud began the old Indian custom of distributing gifts among his tribe.

This was a strong trait of the Indian character. The greater the man and the greater his grief, the more was expected of him. These gifts consisted of horses, blankets, lodges and articles of every conceivable nature, owned by the chief; nothing being reserved. The object of the crying squaws will now be readily understood. They were to share with others the generosity of their chief, and they considered their antics necessary to that end. I am inclined to think that these gifts were given only for effect and afterward returned, for in two weeks Red Cloud seemed to own approximately as much as he had owned before. This is merely a supposition, but I think the facts will prove that I am very nearly correct.

In due time Red Cloud's grief (as in the case of the white man) gradually wore off and he again resumed his usual activities. In a few months we began to give dances at the commissary, Thursray evenings being set apart for this purpose. In order to get the half-breed girls to participate (the full blood girls refused to attend), it was necessary to treat them to a dinner after the dance. The agent prevailed on Red Cloud to attend these dances, which he did, and he took to them as a duck does to water, and enjoyed himself immensely. Ben Tibbetts and I took it upon ourselves to teach him square dances, and he proved a very apt pupil. At first naturally awkward, but he gradually threw off all restraint and entered into the sport heartwhole and enjoyed it as much as the balance of us. The keen enjoyment of those evenings is never to be forgotten. Finally the half-breed boys began coming and raised such havoc with the dinners, for they had abnormal appetites, that we were forced to discontinue by orders from the agent.

Back in the year 1866, Red Cloud had been a prominent leader in the Fort Phil Kearney massacre. Some years after that occurence, he came into Fort Laramie, called on General Smith, who was in command there, and asked him for a basin of water. Much surprised, Smith asked him what he wanted it for. His reply was "To wash the white man's blood from my hands, for I have been up to my arm pits in it." He had reference to the massacre. Smith granted his request, and after washing his hands and arms, Red Cloud promised he would never harm a white man. From that time until his death, he always kept his word, but although he instructed his tribe to do likewise, they were hard to control and occasionally trouble resulted.

While visiting Laramie City, on the line of the Union Pacific Railway, in 1912, I met there my old friend, N. K. Boswell. He informed me that the town of Laramie City was located in 1868, and was the next terminus after Cheyenne. The founders of this town were Ace and Con Moyer. They appointed themselves to the following offices: Ace, justice of the peace, and Con, marshal. They then appointed a man named Big Ned as assistant to Con. Ace then opened a saloon with a large room in the rear which was used as the justice office. A great many murders were committed in this room. The saloon was the rendesvous for railroad laborers. When they were paid their wages they would play against Ace's saloon. If at night they had any money left, they were taken into this room and knocked on the head with an iron bar, and later put in a wagon by Big Steve, hauled two miles from the town, and dumped in a deep, dry gulch, where the wolves would devour them. So many disappeared that the saloon was called the "Bucket of Blood." Finally the citizens became aroused and under the lead of N. K. Boswell, organized themselves into a vigilance committee. One night Ace, Con and Big Steven were rounded up and taken to a partly completed log house, and hanged there by adjusting the rope around their necks, standing them on boxes, and pushing them of into eternity. Thus ended the careers of three bad men. Big Steve requested that his shoes be removed before hanging, as his mother had always said he would die with his shoes on, and he wanted to fool her. The request was granted. Note in the illustration his shoes on the ground. This picture is from an old daguerrotype loaned me by Mr. Boswell, who is still living in Laramie, hale and hearty at the age of 87.

To give the reader some idea of the duties and determination of this man Boswell, as a deputy U. S. marshal, I will relate one circumstance told me by an old-time banker of Laramie City. A very bad character in that country had committed an offense against the U. S. government and the chief marshal, Jeff Carr, sent for Boswell and instructed him to follow and arrest this man, if he had to kill him. If killed, to bring in some evidence of his death. Boswell took the fellow's trail, both being mounted and armed. They were known to be two of the best rifle shots in Wyoming. The criminal was heading for the notorious Jackson Hole in northwestern Wyoming. Boswell knew if he reached there that his chance for capturing the criminal was lost, as no one was ever arrested in that almost unknown, mountainous and wild country. Boswell was well mounted and gained on his quarry rapidly. On the fourth day he was six hours behind him at a ranch kept by a Canadian Frenchman, a friend of Boswell's. On questioning this man, he told Boswell that his man slept in his ranch that night, and had left two hours previous to Boswell's arrival. Boswell changed horses and proceeded on his way. The Frenchman wanted to accompany him. Boswell informed him that having his family to care for, he had better remain at his ranch. After Boswell left, "Frenchy," knowing how desperate the criminal was, saddled his horse and cutting the corners across country, managed to get in advance of the hunted. Finally Boswell discovered his man. The man also saw Boswell. They both dismounted, getting behind rocks for shelter. It was now a battle of wits. Boswell resorted to the old trick of putting his hat on a stick and putting it in sight in hopes of drawing the other's fire. But the trick did not work. Presently Boswell heard a gun shot, and was surprised that it came from the north. He was amazed to see a man in the distance, mounted, waving his hat to him to come on. After some time, he realized that it was his friend "Frenchy." Cautiously going to him, he was informed that he had shot the criminal through the head. Both going over to the spot, found it to be a fact. It being too far to take the body to Cheyenne, Boswell decapitated it and took the head to Cheyenne as evidence. Those were trying days in the West., and required men of nerve and steel. Boswell was of that caliber.

CHAPTER XIV.

MORE BAD INDIANS—THE BAD INDIAN BOY—BEEF
CATTLE ISSUES—POWDER AND LEAD VERSUS GEW-
GAWS — INDIAN COWARDICE — OLD THUNDER'S
TOSS-UP—SIOUX ENUMERATION—THE PUPPY DOG
FEAST AND WHAT IT ACCOMPLISHED.

IT would take a long time to enumerate all of the
bad Indians and boys. An Indian named "Bad
Hand"—the name given on account of a defective
hand, had a son about ten years old. One day near
noon-time, as we were going to dinner in the slab-
house heretofore referred to, the stockade not yet
being finished, this boy slipped up behind an old man
named Evans, a carpenter, and with an arrow from a
small bow, shot him in the back, just below the
shoulder blade, the arrow penetrating his back about
six inches. I was a few steps behind the boy when he
shot. Evans fell, badly hurt. The arrow shaft sticking from his back about eight inches. After the
shooting this boy ran away laughing and the Indians,
young and old, made great fun of it. I want to
mentioned here that the Sioux Indians encourage their
boys in everything that was bad, and taught them
from infancy to hate the white man. I have seen
little children unable to walk grin at a white man in
a hideous way, showing their intense hatred while yet
unable to talk.

We carried Evans into the bunk house and in
trying to pull the arrow out, pulled the shaft out of
the point, which was made of hoop iron. We had no
doctor there at the time, and it was a question how to
extract this point. Monahan, using his knife, cut into
the flesh, then taking a pair of nippers, he extracted
the point, old Evans howling for mercy. The Indians
remarked that he was not brave. We fixed the old

man up the best we could and shipped him down to Fort Laramie, where he died from the wound. Bad Hand praised his boy for the deed and called him a great brave and thus the matter ended.

After being on the Agency for some time, I was given charge of the cattle herd. At this particular time we issued to the Sioux one thousand head of cattle per month, five hundred on the first and five hundred on the fifteenth. Leaving the agency on the twenty-fifth, my duty was to ride forty-five miles to the beef contractor's range. With me there was one white man and twenty Indians. On arriving at the range, I gave to Mr. Bozler, who had the cattle contract, an order issued by the agent for one thousand head. On receiving the cattle, I receipted for them and drove them toward the agency about twenty miles. Early the following morning, we would complete the drive to the agency. The object of having those Indians with me was to protect the cattle from northern Indians who did not belong on the agency. Without this protection they would rush into the herd, selecting cows which were with calf, as an unborn calf, either cow or buffalo, was a great delicacy with the Sioux.

On arriving at the agency, we would rest the cattle up until the first and then make the issue. We drove them into a large corral, two mounted men accompanying them. As an exit, we built a gate large enough for a steer to go through. Over the top of this gate was a wide plank on which I stood with a long pole with a spike in the end of it. On the prairie outside of this corral were approximately five thousand Indians, squaws, children and dogs. Joe Bessnet, with the commissary clerk and the principal Indians of the various tribes, stood on a platform near the gate. The interpreter would call out, "Young, let out twenty head for Red Cloud's band." I would open the gate and the mounted men would force the cattle out. I would count them and when the required number was out, would punch the others back and close the gate.

Indians belonging to Red Cloud's band would then attack the cattle, using guns, bow and arrows, and also spears, until they killed them all. This was repeated until the issue was complete, and I assure you that this was a gala sight and a great deal of fun was witnessed. Many of the cattle were wounded, and the Indians, children and squaws being dressed in gaudy colors, the wounded steers would attack them. Then there was a scampering to get under cover, some crawling up on the corral, others running in all directions, children crying and Indians laughing. Then came the squaws part. As soon as the cattle were pronounced dead, the squaws, children and dogs gathered around the carcass, first skinning it, then cutting out the tongue. The buck who had killed the animal, sat there on horse back waiting for the tail of the hide to he handed him, with which he started on a dead run for the trading store. There he exchanged it for powder and lead and a few beads for the squaws.

In the meantime, the squaws were removing the entrails. The older ones putting one of the small intestines in their mouths and chewing while the process was going on, the dogs coming in for their share as well. They would allow nothing to go to waste; and even now I can picture them as they appeared at that particular time. All were as busy as bees, chewing away, the offal continually running from the corners of their mouths. It was sickening sight. They then cut the flesh in long strips, loading it crosswise on their pony's backs with all they could carry. They would then start for their permanent camps. On arrival there they would hang this flesh on poles with crotch sticks for uprights. This was for the purpose of sun-drying it. A portion of this was handled in the following manner for future use. They took the flesh and with large knives chopped it up very fine, mixing with it either plums, cherries or berries, whichever was in season, using the entire fruit, which they pounded together, giving it the appearance of pulp. Then they took a green bladder and filled it with this material, tying it tightly with a thong.

When an Indian had a long journey to make, he took with him one or two of those bladders, and it is wonderful how long they could subsist on this material.

Again referring to issue day, I wish to cite a comical occurrence. Before issuing the cattle early in the morning, Ben Tibbetts would come down to the corral with his Winchester gun, and all the discarded old bucks and squaws trailing behind him, as these were the people he had to care for. Entering the corral, Ben would shoot down twenty head of cattle and with a mule would drag them out on the prairie. The squaws and old men would skin them, remove the entrails, which became their property. He then would have the beef hauled to the Agency, part of it being kept for the use of the white men and the balance issued daily to the old men and squaws. Among these old men was an Indian named Thunder, bent over with age, until his hands were not over a foot from the ground, and when he moved he looked as though he might be walking on four legs. This old fellow was a hideous sight.

It was a custom when Ben would shoot a steer that the first old Indian or squaw to get to the animal, was entitled to the tongue. They would watch Ben closely and when he shot and the steer fell, they would all rush and many, many fights they had among one another making claim for this tongue. Ben, in his commanding way, would decide who was entitled to the tongue, and that settled it.

Ben in one instance shot a steer and the ball must have hit him a glancing blow. He fell all right, and old Thunder being close by, got there first, and with three others was about to turn the head over to extract the tongue, when up jumped Mr. Steer. Thunder, being less active than the others, started for the side of the corral. The steer seeing him, rushed at him, throwing him with his horns up against the fence, knocking old Thunder out. After this occurrence they were very careful to know that a steer was truly dead before they went near him.

At these issues the very young children came in for their fun; while we were issuing the cattle, they would shoot arrows from their small bows into them. The steer hit, would, of course, bellow, which would create a great deal of laughter. They would continue to do this as we had no power to stop them, until toward the end those having been hit would attack the men and horses. Then, as it was impossible for those men mounted to stay in there, the interpreter would tell me to let them all go. He would then harangue the Indians, telling them that we were going to do so, and that they belonged to those who could kill them. They would arrange themselves on the outside of the gate and the moment I opened it, it would seem as if Bedlam had turned loose. I would not attempt to describe the excitement of this scene. This ended issue day at Red Cloud Agency.

In addition to this cattle issue, we had a commissary issue once a month. On this day we issued flour, bacon, beans, coffee, sugar, molasses and corn. This was another gala day, Indians coming from all directions to participate in it. At this particular time, the Sioux would not eat bread, or rather, would not make it. They did not seem to understand what flour was for. They would accept the flour, the old squaws carrying it out on the prairie, dump it in a pile, shake the sack well and retain it. They were particularly fond of flour sacks.

I wish to state here that the squaws did all the laborious work. The greatest disgrace that could befall an Indian was to do any kind of manual labor. The squaws did it all. Referring again to the bread and seeing them continually dumping this flour, I remarked to Dr. Seville, the agent, that I thought I could teach them to use this flour for making bread. He replied, "I will let you try it on next issue day." I did so in the following manner: I had our cook bake up in Dutch ovens in the presence of a great many squaws, about six pones of bread. The squaws looked on with a great deal of curiosity at this operation. I then got a small keg of molasses, knocking the head in, I then broke off a large piece of bread, and dipping it down into the molasses, I ate it. A hideous looking old squaw stepped from the crowd and very cautiously approached me. I dipped another piece, offered it to her. She refused. I then took another bite of it, smacking my lips; then dipping it again, I offered it to her, and to my surprise she snatched it from my hands and ate it ravenously. They all then rushed for the bread and molasses, eating it all up, and from that time on I never knew any flour to go to waste.

Dr. Seville received an order from the Interior Department to get in some manner or other a count on the number of Indians on the agency. I wish the reader to bear in mind that this agency was two hundred miles from civilization and that there were but twenty-one of us white men employed there, and if a Sioux objected to anything, that ended it as far as we were concerned.

The agent was in a great quandry how to approach them to get this count, for at this particular time he well knew that they were drawing more rations than they were entitled to, and also knew that the Interior Department wanted this count so as to arrange for their future rations. The agent finally concluded to give them a great feast to make "their hearts good," or as we would express it, to put them in good humor. He notified us boys to get evergreens and decorate the immense commissary and not to tell the Indians why we were doing so, as he wanted to surprise them. After the decorations were complete, he then notified the prominent chiefs that the great father in Washington had ordered him to give them a great feast.

One of the Indian delicacies was young pups. The agent had the old squaws for about a week gathering up all the pups they could, bringing them into the agency. Ben Tibbetts took charge of the preparation for this feast. On the day appointed he had the old squaws build numerous fires, and using large camp kettles, stew these pups, making many, many gallons of it. When all was ready, the white men carried it in tin receptacles holding about a quart, and we acted as waiters, the old squaws dishing it out and we white men serving it. I don't know any time that I was as completely worn out as I was after that feast.

After they had eaten all they cared to, the agent, through the chief interpreter, addressed them, informing them that the great father in Washington wanted to know how many children he had to take care of the next year, and asked them if they would allow him to count them. To simplify the matter, he figured on averaging them five to a lodge. This would hasten the work as we would then only have to count their lodges. When Bissnet interpreted this to them, there was a great commotion. However, Red Cloud and other powerful chiefs, who were seated on the floor in front, quieted them.

When order had been restored, Red Cloud rose gradually from a sitting position and when erect he put out his right hand with the palm toward the North. I don't believe a finer physique than his ever stood on two feet. He was over six feet tall, perfectly built and was Nature's own child. He then replied to the agent in a long speech, giving a history of the Sioux from his childhood up to that time, stating how they had fought their way from the far North; how they came in to be civilized like the white man; how they had conquered and driven other tribes before them; how bad white men enticed his people to buy liquor; how they debauched their children, stole their lands and horses, and now cooped them up in a little corner of their vast domain; and now the great father wanted to know how many there were of them left. He then said, "Yes, we will let you count our lodges." This pleased the agent so that he clapped his hands, jumping around like a child with glee. Red Cloud watched him, not saying a word until the agent quieted down, then he continued, "but in return for this, we want the great father to issue to each grown Indian a Winchester gun and forty rounds of ammunition. The change on the agent's face was indescribable, for at that time the Government were thinking seriously of disarming them, and they knew it. The poor agent had nothing more to say. The Indians arose, walking in single file out of the commissary, and the agent with his interpreter retired to his quarters. This was a case of love's labor lost, for the lodges were never counted.

CHAPTER XV.

THE SIOUX LANGUAGE—RISE OF THE TOBACCO HABIT
—THE YOUNG SQUAW AND HER DOMESTIC HABITS
—COURTSHIP AND MARRIAGE—SIOUX THEORY OF
ORIGIN OF INDIANS—A SIOUX HALF-BREED'S ES-
CAPE FROM CHEYENNE JAIL.

MUCH has been said and written about the Sioux language. It is quite difficult for an interpreter to translate English into Sioux or Sioux into English, as the Sioux language has few words compared with English, and interpreting either one to the other is by no means easy. In fact, the interpreter adds or re-tracts, to suit the occasion. For instance, if he does not exactly understand just what the Sioux wishes understood, he in his judgment tells what he thinks would be satisfactory to both parties concerned, and in doing this it creates many misunderstandings in their future dealings. Another trait of the Sioux, if he see anything new to him, by some action of this object he gives it a Sioux name. As an illustration, the first sawmill that they saw in operation they called it a slush lush la tepee. The slush lush part of this name was the noise made by the exhaust pipe where the steam escaped, making the sound slush lush. Tepee in Sioux means a house, tent or lodge, or anything one might live in.

I have known commissioners being sent out to the Agency by the Government to make new treaties with the Sioux, and the interpretation through the interpre-ter was very misleading when they attempted to put them into practical operation. This was caused as stated above by the interpreter misquoting what the Indian and commissioners intended, thus causing a great deal of trouble.

When I first went on the Agency, the Indian was not a tobacco smoker. They smoked in their Indian pipes what was called Kinna Kinick. This was made from a red willow. With their knives they would scrape off the red part very carefully, then scrape the main part, which they dried in the sun. This caused it to curl up similar to shavings. After it was thoroughly dried, they chopped it up very fine and put it into a little beaded bag made of buckskin. Their pipes in which they smoked this material were of a soft clay that they dug from bluffs. It was of a red color. They dried this, which made it very hard. They then, with very crude tools, a knife being the principal one, shaped into a pipe of various designs, and on the bowls of these pipes they made figures, generally a deer or a bear. They then inserted in the bowl a long stem. How they bored the hole through this stem, I do not know. This stem was also carved; some of them were flat and others round. In smoking they would take two or three draws and pass it to the Indian sitting to their left, and keep doing so until the pipe was empty.

In due time they began the use of tobacco. They first had the white man roll it in paper, making a cigarette, and they finally became very expert in making them themselves. However, the older Indians stuck to their pipes, but the younger ones became inveterate cigarette smokers, and I never recollect at any time seeing them smoking a pipe containing tobacco.

Many of the young squaws before marriage were very pretty and coquettish, painted and dressed up in gaudy colors; many of them wearing fine beaded work and other ornaments too numerous to mention. Thus attired they made it a practice to come around the Agency in large numbers in the afternoons, meeting the young bucks and exchanging signs of admiration. They had a peculiar mode of courtship. The young buck who wished to marry had the courting done for him in the following manner:

His most intimate friend would run after and catch a young squaw, throwing a blanket over her, which covered them both. This was called blanketing. While holding her in close embrace, he would tell her of all the good traits of his friend; how rich he was in horses, buffalo robes, etc.; how daring and brave he was, and what a fine brave he would make for her. During this blanketing act the prospective groom would stand at a respective distance, arms folded, silent and erect as a statute. (I wonder how many white men would have cared to go through court- ship in this manner. I think they would have drawn the line at the part the friend was to play). If she consented to have his friend, he released her and she ran like a deer to her lodge and father. The brave then erected a lodge, fitting it out with the necessary cooking utensils, and immediately began negotiations with her father. He would lead a pony up to her lodge and himself stand there for a limited time. If her father did not appear, he would bring another pony and continue bringing ponies and robes until her father appeared, leading her by the hand. This was a sign that full value had been tendered for the girl.

This simple ceremony of marriage was all that was required among the Indians. The groom and bride would then start for his lodge in single file, the squaw in front. She was now his beast of burden for life. The Indians were polygamous, many of them having as many as six wives. Oft times these wives were jealous of each other, and it was not unusual for them to settle their differences by engaging in desperate fights, in which knives were freely used. On these occasions the brave would take no part, simply looking on with the greatest unconcern.

I have often wondered why scientists have never investigated the origin of the Sioux. I have my own ideas, which have been growing stronger since I came to the Pacific Coast, and am quite sure that the Sioux originally came from the Orient, and were of Asiatic origin. Their characteristics were very similar to those of the Chinese in many respects. Indians, on being questioned, have proved to have poor memories, their childhood being the limit of their remembrance. The oldest of them have invariably conveyed the meaning by signs that they came from the north, and I shall always think they originally came from China, which might easily be conceded to, as the Behring Sea of North America and Siberia joining China, they could easily have landed in North America in canoes, then becoming meat and fish eaters, they would naturally grow more stalwart than the Chinaman. Their features were much the same as also their pigeon English. Their funeral ceremonies were identical in form, food in large quantities being taken to the graves for the dead and crying being one of their common customs, the only exception being that the Indian deposited his dead in trees.

In the spring of 1872, a young halfbreed Sioux, named Tuscon Kessler, while under the influence of bad whiskey, rode up to a cabin situated on the Laramie River above Fort Laramie, and calling to the door an old, harmless Mexican, who followed the occupation of a wood chopper, shot and killed him. Later on he was captured and taken to Cheyenne, where he was tried, convicted and sentenced to be hung. About six o'clock in the evening previous to the execution, he made his escape. This was a very mysterious occurrence, no one seeming to know how he escaped and it is surmised that the death-watch, in connection with some other official, had been paid a sum of money to help this fellow escape.

When Kessler left the jail, he was shackled at the feet, the chain being about six inches long. He was also handcuffed. In the rear of this jail was a stable, where the sheriff kept his coal black saddle horse, considered the best in Wyoming. How he succeeded in bridling this horse and getting on his bare back, no one ever knew. If he did, he never told. Lying on his stomach, his feet being over the loins of the horse, his hands would naturally be over his weathers, and in this way he could hold the bridle rein and guide the horse. At about six thirty o'clock in the morning, he arrived at the Platte River, which was ninety miles distant from Cheyenne. Swimming the horse across the river, he arrived at Nick Jennesse's ranch. Nick released his feet and hands by breaking the shackles, and furnished him a fresh horse on which he continued on north and joined the Sioux Indians. This Jennessee was what was termed a squaw man and was living there with a Sioux squaw. As stated previously, any Sioux or Sioux half-breed committing any depredation south of the Platte River, was free if he could get to the north side before being captured, as the sheriff or soldiers could not follow him under existing conditions at that time. In 1874, while I was employed on Red Cloud Agency, I saw and talked with this fellow a great many times. He was dressed in Indian attire completely; his face painted in many colors, and was wearing the breech-clout, blanket and moccasins. The authorities offered a standing reward of one thousand dollars for his capture, dead or alive.

In 1878, a young lieutenant stationed at Camp Robinson, came over to Red Cloud Agency in an ambulance, accompanied by four soldiers. Kessler, with some other Indians was sitting on the bank of the White River, when the ambulance stopped, and an old Indian stepped up to the officer and in his pigeon English told him that one of the Indians was Kessler, at the same time pointing a finger at the latter. Kessler, always on the alert, witnessed the action and immediately started to run, the officer shot at him, striking him in the left hip and disabling him. Before the Indians standing around could regain their senses, the officer called to the ambulance driver and throwing Kessler in the wagon, took him to Camp Robinson, and under a strong guard of soldiers that night, started with him for Cheyenne, arriving there in safety and turning him over to Jeff Carr, who was sheriff at the time, and in a few days receiving the reward, returned to Camp Robinson. This was a very nervy act, and it is miraculous that he got away with it. They then tried to get Kessler to confess as to how he made his escape, but he was true blue and would not do so.

In a short time Kessler was hanged and while standing on the scaffold, the sheriff asked him if he had any request to make. He replied,

"Yes. The white men in this country whom I hate, yourself included, have gloated over the fact that I would die with my boots on," and at the same time asked the sheriff to remove them, which he did. Kessler then said, "Let her go." They put on the black cap, after adjusting the noose, sprung the trap and thus ended the career of a very bad half-breed Sioux.

After the Sioux war of 1876, much was talked and written about that famous scout, Frank Geruard, whom I knew well. Many have the idea that he was a Sioux Indian. This is a mistake, as I happen to know his history, as told to me by himself.

In 1860, a lady named Mrs. Peal, the wife of an army officer, was in Honolulu for her health. There she made the acquaintance of the parents of this boy. She became fascinated with the little fellow and adopted him, bringing him with her to Fort Laramie. Two months after her arrival the child was playing

in the rear of her quarters, when a Sioux chief named
Crazy Horse saw the child, and no one being in sight,
he threw a blanket over the youngster and rode off
with him to the north, to his camp.

This Indian was a powerful chief and becoming
attached to the child, kept him prisoner there until
1876, when Geruard escaped and coming to Fort
Laramie, offered his services to General Crook. Crook
refused him, thinking him a Sioux Indian. Geruard
then went to General Smith, who was in command at
the post, and told him who he was. Smith immediately called on General Crook, advising him to employ
Geruard, adding that he (Geruard) was very bitter
toward the Sioux, knew their habits and customs, and
also knew very much of their country. Crook accepted him. Later on Miles succeeded Crook and
retained the services of Geruard and found him one of
the most valuable men in that capacity, and to this
man Geruard is due the credit of the final surrender
of the Sioux.

It is said that Geruard approached General Miles
one day, saying to him: "If you will follow a plan that
I give you, we can corral and kill, or force, these
fellows to surrender in thirty days. Miles asked him
how. Geruard replied, "Move your troops rapidly by
railroad"—the Northern Pacific being constructed
through Montana—"and then get light draft steamers
on the upper Missouri River and I will show you where
to station your troops." The Sioux were now retreating north after the Custer massacre. He explained to Miles that the Indians having their families
with them would be compelled to travel through
certain passes in the mountains and cross rivers at
certain places, and that he knew them all. Miles
turning around, remarked, "Trash!" But in thirty
days he did just as Geruard had suggested; Miles

taking the credit to himself, for what was accomplished.

When the advance Sioux arrived at these passes and river fords, they found soldiers there and returned to report the fact to their chiefs. The Indians then realized that they were corraled and the only thing left them to do was to delegate three of their prominent chiefs, under a flag of truce, to make the best terms possible with Miles. Thus terminated the Sioux War of 1876.

The last I heard of Geruard, he was living in obscurity on the Laramie River, some twenty miles above Fort Laramie, old and penniless. And it is a shame that this great government does not provide a pension for such faithful servants.

CHAPTER XVI.

**MORE ABOUT THE INDIANS—SIOUX WARFARE—DE-
SCRIPTION OF A SIOUX WAR DANCE—THE KOO
STICK EXPLAINED—HOW SCALPING IS DONE—THE
SIOUX SUN DANCE DESCRIBED—SUN WORSHIPPERS
SELECTING THE VIRGINS—HORRIBLE TORTURE OF
YOUNG BRAVES.**

I WILL describe one of the Sioux war dances,
which was held in the Agency stockade some
time after the murder of the old men and women
of the Pawnee tribe previously referred to:

The Sioux had many scalps and carried them
tied to the chin straps of their ponies' bridles or
arranged them on long spears. They were all painted
in their war paint, all mounted, the most prominent
Indians sitting in a very large circle, and on the outside of this circle were the squaws, children and old
men. One of these young bucks would ride his horse
into the circle, suddenly stopping. This horse had
many hand marks painted on his body, generally in
white. Many of these marks in close proximity to
the rider. This was to show what desperate en-
counters he had had with the enemy; how close he
was to him. These marks meaning the enemy's hand
prints. He would then tell how he shot the enemy
and how he scalped him, at the same time pointing
to the scalp. The old Indians sitting in the circle
would applaud them; the old and young squaws doing
likewise.

After a number of these young bucks had gone
through this ceremony, the old squaws would start
their war cry. All the Indians present would rise to
their feet, forming a great circle. A young buck
would then place on end a spear with a scalp attached,
the old squaws beating their tom toms, they would

then begin their dance, going through all kinds of antics, which at times were very comical. They would continue this for hours, until they became exhausted. These fellows are great braggarts, for as a fact they had no trouble in killing these poor old Pawnees.

For the benefit of the reader, I will explain one of their characteristics. Every young Sioux warrior when on murder bent, carries what is called a koo stick. It is about twelve inches long. This is used for the following purpose:

If two young Sioux should both shoot and kill an enemy, the one getting to him first and touching him with this koo stick gets the credit of killing him and is entitled to his scalp. When telling of their exploits, they term it counting their koos, meaning by that the number they have killed.

All Indians wear what they term their scalp lock. This is made at the top of the head of a space about the size of a silver dollar. They gather the hair up and plait it, its length being about six inches. To this they usually attach a colored feather. In scalping the enemy, they seize the scalp lock and with the point of their scalping knife, cut the scalp in this space mentioned and with a sudden motion pull it from the head. Were this victim a white man, they would sometimes take his entire hair, then cutting it up into three or four pieces, claim that they had killed three or four white men, while as a fact they had killed but one. When they returned to their camp, the squaws dressed these scalps, using almost the same process that they would in tanning a buffalo hide. This preserves it. The young buck then attaches it to his person and when they have their war dances, exposes it as I have previously described.

In my time on the Agency, the Sioux were sun worshippers and once a year, usually in the month of May, they held their sun dance. The whole Sioux nation attended this as it was a religious ceremony with them. They were all decked out in their best bib and tucker and were a wonderful sight to look upon. Early in the morning before sunrise, they congregated on the west side of a long, high ridge, when suddenly one of their chiefs would harangue them. They would then lie down on their stomachs close to the earth and as the sun appeared, they would gradually rise with it, and when the sun had risen clear of the ride, they were all standing erect. I never could understand how they kept pace in rising with the sun, but they did nevertheless. They would then bow very low three times, holding their arms erect with their palms toward the sun. Suddenly there was a great commotion and a hideously dressed Indian, mounted and making motions at the assembled Indians, ten or fifteen of them would suddenly step out in front and shoot with their guns at this fellow. He was their great medicine man and was bullet proof.

Ben Tibbetts and I witnessed this act and after they had quit shooting, none of the shots having struck the object, Ben remarked, "I would like a crack at that fellow with my Winchester," and I assure you they would have to make a new medicine man. It is a question whether they shot to kill or not. However, the medicine man was unharmed. In a few moments another one appeared. He passed through the same ordeal without being injured. Then four others appeared at intervals, all passing safely.

The next part of the ceremony was the virgin pole scene. The Sioux kept a record each year of their virgins. To do so the old squaws erected a large pole, the young girls forming themselves in a line, each one putting on an apron made of deer skin. An old squaw then handed her a small hatchet. The young bucks in the meantime had formed themselves in line, extending, I should judge, a quarter mile, leaving a space in the center large enough for the young girls to pass through. One of the chiefs then gave the order and the procession of young girls passed up the line to the virgin pole, each one taking her apron with one hand by the corner, and if she was what she represented herself to be, she cut a chip from the virgin pole, which dropped into her apron. She then took a position, waiting until the entire number passed up the line.

Returning through the line to the starting point, if the young squaw was not what she had represented herself to be, a young buck, knowing so, would expose her. She was then taken by the old squaws and severely whipped. On the other hand, if she were what she represented herself to be, the squaws made a great ado over her, giving her many presents. Just how they registered them, I do not know, but I do know it to be a fact that they kept a complete record of them.

The next ceremony was the torture of young bucks who wanted to become braves. The squaws again erecting a pole, tying from it near the top long thongs similar to our May pole. The young men then walked out, each with a knife in his hand, some cutting themselves on the breast just through the skin and separating the skin from the flesh, then attaching the thong. Others cut themselves in a like manner in the back, inserting a thong and tying to it a buffalo head or beef head. Then they began dancing in a circle, pulling against the pole until they tore the thong from the flesh. Others with the heads attached, danced around until the thong was torn out. The old men in the meantime both praised and criticised their bravery. They were then graded off as full-fledged warriors. Those going through the greatest amount of torture were pronounced great braves, the others, merely braves.

The next ceremony was the piercing of their children's ears. The squaws would sit down in large circles with a piece of hide on their knee, and with a sharp pointed knife in hand, would motion the children to them and laying their ear on the piece of hide, would pierce the child's ear at the top and bottom. And it is wonderful to state that not one of those children uttered so much as a whimper.

After going through these ceremonies, the assembly scattered in all directions, some runing pony races, others gambling, others running foot races, Indian against Indian, or an Indian against a horse. The young bucks playing with the young squaws and ending up with a great jollification and a feast.

CHAPTER XVII.

MORE CHARACTERISTICS OF THE SIOUX—HOW THE IN-
TERIOR DEPARTMENT LOST CONTROL OF THE
SIOUX—UNWRITTEN HISTORY—MURDER OF FRANK
APPLETON—ONE TEAR SHED BY RED CLOUD—
ORIGIN OF CAMP ROBINSON—THE JENNY EXPEDI-
TION OR "GOLD IN THE BLACK HILLS."

I AM now drawing near the time when I left the
Agency, and wish to mention two characteristics
of the Sioux. Few readers of this book have any
idea of the origin of the heliograph. Before my
time among those people they carried on their
persons a round piece of polished silver, and when
they wanted to get into communication with others
of their kind, they would ascend a high hill and with
this piece of polished silver, would signal with dots
and dashes the same as used by our present telegraphic code, this being accomplished by the reflection
of the sun. In time it would be answered by other
Indians a long distance away. Later on and during
my time among them, they substituted a piece of
looking glass and one could not find a grown Sioux
without this piece of glass on his person. In cloudy
weather they substituted for this, grass smoke. They
would build a fire on the hilltop, immediately smother
it with grass, then holding a blanket or buffalo robe
over it by the four corners until it was filled with
smoke. If they wished to signal a dot, they would let
out a small quantity of smoke. If a dash, they would
let out a larger quantity. If they wished to signal
by night, they would build a fire, covering it in the
same manner and for a dot, they would quickly expose
the fire and for a dash, a longer exposure. Their
telegraphic code may not have been so complete as
ours, but their system was certainly the same. I am

sure that the credit of the heliograph should be given
to General Custer, as he had a large experience with
the Indians and was conversant with their habits and
would be the most likely one to have reported this
signalling, when the War Department, by experiments,
invented the heliograph. This was used largely by our
signal corps on the plains and elsewhere prior to the
discovery of wireless telegraphy.

The Sioux, as previously mentioned, were great
braggarts and dreamers. I will cite you an instance
of this characteristic. In January, 1874, they had
very deep snows in Wyoming and Nebraska. This
made traffic difficult for freighting teams. At this
time a man named Charles Clay had the contract for
freighting the supplies to Red Cloud Agency from
Cheyenne. His transportation was by ox teams. For
about thirty days he was unable to get through to the
Agency with these supplies. Consequently we were
cempletely out of everything. The Indians in the
morning would ride out on a high hill, sitting there
until almost dark, looking to the south in hopes of
seeing these teams coming. They would come into the
Agency at night and report to the agent that they
saw heaps of teams coming. At first this was good
news to us, but in a couple of days no teams arrived.
They would then repeat the operation, bringing in the
same news. They would keep this up for several days,
and as a fact, the teams did not arrive for fifteen
days. What I wish to impress the reader with is,
that the Indian having this supply train in mind, and
not wanting to report anything but good news, really
imagined he saw the teams, and the oftener he went
on this hilltop, the more he believed he saw them.
Before they finally arrived, the Indians were compelled to kill their ponies and eat them.

The reader has probably read or heard of the Sioux
War of 1876. But few know the actual causes that

led up to it. In the month of March, 1875, a young man arrived on the Agency named Frank Appleton. His father having preceded him to the Agency to teach the Sioux how to farm and was termed "Boss Farmer." Frank was the nephew of Dr. Seville. Upon his arrival there he was appointed chief clerk to the agent, Otis Johnson having retired. Before coming to the Agency and while in Cheyenne, he broke his leg and came to the Agency using crutches. We all liked him very much and talked with him a great deal about his eastern home. He was from Sioux City, Iowa. He told us in conversation that he did not want to come out there, but that his father and Seville insisted on his coming, and while in Cheyenne before breaking his leg he had a dream that something awful was going to happen, and while on the Agency he begged his father and uncle to allow him to return to his home, also telling them of his dream, and they laughed at him. Consequently, he remained.

On April 1st Dr. Seville went down to Spotted Tail Agency, which was forty miles north of Red Cloud Agency. His business there was to confer with their agent in regard to an order from Washington to formulate some plans to disarm the Sioux. About three o'clock in the afternoon of this day an Indian arrived on the Agency. He was not one of our regular Indians, but belonged up north. He had just arrived from the Platte River and stated that a white man had killed his brother down there and that in retaliation he was going to kill one of us white men before he went north. Joe Bessnet, the chief interpreter, hearing this from the Indians, conversed with the fellow. He then warned us white men not to go on the outside of the stockade that evening for fear this fellow might carry out his threat. This stockade was built of lumber fourteen feet high, the lumber being three inches thick. The entrance had two large gates that swung against a center post and when the gates were closed, they were hooked on the inside with hooks and staples. When darkness came, we closed the gates. During the day one of the carpenters carelessly left a ladder on the outside. This Indian, about two o'clock the following morning, ascended this ladder and dropped inside the stockade, and then unfastened the gates. Then going to Appleton's sleeping quarters, which was the nearest building to the gates, knocked on the door. Appleton got up, putting on his slippers, cap and long ulster, stepped outside and asked the Indian what he wanted. The Indian replied something in the Sioux language. Appleton not understanding Sioux and knowing that Billy Hunter, the assistant interpreter, was sleeping in the quarters with myself, Mike Dunne and Paddy Simmons, turned his back to the Indian and made but a few steps toward these quarters when the Indian shot him, using a Winchester rifle, hitting him just under the left shoulder blade.

The report of the gun awoke us boys. We hurriedly dressed and going out of the door, saw Appleton on his hands and knees trying to get up. When he heard us, he said, "Come quick, boys, I am shot." We hurried to him and carrying him into his bedroom, he told us that he knew he was going to die. A young doctor had arrived on the Agency the day before, and we woke him up, telling him that Appleton was severely wounded, but he was so frightened that we could not get him out of his room. Billy Hunter then ran down to Red Cloud's camp, which was but a short distance away, telling him what had happened. Red Cloud then set Indian runners to Man Afraid of His Horses and Chief Little Wound's camp. They all three came into the room where Frank lay, Red Cloud sitting down on the side of the bed near Frank's head, took him by the hand, patting it on the back, and with head bowed and with tears trickling down his cheeks, said: "It is too bad. You are a good man. Bad Indian live up north." A few minutes later Appleton died.

This was the first tear I ever knew an Indian to shed. Red Cloud having lost his son previous to this, the memory of which came back to him with great force and melted his Indian heart to tears. Mike Dunne immediately started on horseback for Spotted Tail Agency to inform Seville. When daylight came, Indians, young and old, crowded into the stockade in great numbers. Many of them were dressed in their war paint and under great excitement. About two o'clock in the afternoon Seville arrived from Spotted Tail Agency. The leading Indians then held a great council with him which ended by their telling him that they were afraid they could not control their young men as they were very greatly excited.

I neglected to say that in the construction of this stockade, they built in the southeast corner a high cupola, where one could go and get an unobstructed view for miles. The excitement became so great that Joe Bassnet called Ben Tibbetts to one side, telling him in Sioux to take us men up in this cupola, and to remain there until he told us that it was safe to come out. Ben did so. We then took sacks of flour and other food, including water, into the cupola, and with the flour built a barricade. We had but one gun up there, that being a Winchester (the one used by Ben for shooting cattle). There we remained for four days and nights. I could not describe the great excitement going on among the Indians. They came from all directions, the chiefs all sitting in council, trying to decide what was best to do. They held the agent as a hostage until the decision was made. The younger Indians wanted to burn the Agency, kill us white men, and go north.

American Horse, previously spoken of, made the Indians a final talk, telling them if they were brave and wanted to fight the white man that they could go down to Fort Laramie on the Platte River and find plenty of them, including the soldiers, but they must not harm us white men on the Agency; that some of us were married to their people, and were building them an Agency and treating them kindly. This seemed to quiet them. A white man living outside of the stockade with a squaw as a wife—a squaw man, as we termed them—was very much excited and mounting his horse, rode to Fort Laramie in great haste. On arriving there, he told General Smith, who was in command, that the Indians had killed all us white men and had burned the Agency and had gone north on the war path. General Smith immediately telegraphed General Crook, who was in command of the Department of the Platte, with headquarters at Omaha, Nebraska. General Crook informed the War Department at Washington of these conditions. The War Department immediately transferred the Sioux Indians from the Interior Department to the War Department. Crook was then ordered to Fort Laramie, where he organized what was termed the Crook expedition. Three days after the death of Appleton the Indians furnished an escort for the body to Fort Laramie, the doctor accompanying the remains. From there they shipped the body to his home. This showing conclusively that his presentment had come true. Without a question of doubt, the killing of this young man was the true cause of the Sioux War of 1876.

After four days in this cupola, Bessnet informed us that we could go back to our work as all was safe. We all gave American Horse credit for saving our lives. The following day, myself and two others left the Agency for Fort Laramie. We knew that something was going to happen as Appleton, at the time he was killed, was really acting agent, and we knew the government would not stand for this killing. When we arrived at Fort Laramie, all was ex-excitement there; soldiers being equipped, six-mule teams being assembled for transportation purposes, soldiers arriving from Fort D. A. Russell. We immediately made application for a teamster's job and had no trouble in securing one.

To explain more fully regarding conditions existing between the Interior Department and the Military Department regarding the Sioux before the death of Frank Appleton on Red Cloud Agency, I will cite one instance. One bright day in 1873, the horses of K Company, 2nd Cavalry, were out on herd near the Post Fort Laramie, guarded by two cavalry soldiers, when five Sioux Indians rushed in between the Post and the horses and ran them off, taking the soldiers with the horses, getting across the Platte River before they could stop them. The soldiers they stripped of their clothing and sent them back to the Post naked. These horses the Government never did recover as they could not cross the Platte River after them, by virtue of the Sioux treaty. I saw many of these horses on the Agency when I worked there. This expedition verifies the fact that the killing of Appleton changed all treaty relations with the Sioux, and proves that this expedition was the first step in the Sioux war of 1876.

In three days, with ten companies of soldiers, General Crook in command, part being cavalry, we started for the Agency. There were one hundred six-mule teams, and I assure you it was a beautiful sight to look this assembly over. The six-mule teams traveling four abreast across the prairie, cavalry as the advance guard and cavalry as the rear guard. The infantry marched in single file on the outside, also riding in the wagons. In due time we arrived on the Agency and found nothing there except some old bucks and old squaws, the balance of the Indians having gone north, knowing that this expedition was coming to the Agency. The agent and the boys there, were of course, delighted to see us. We camped there for about ten days. Then they established, about three miles from the Agency, Fort Robinson—at that time called "Camp Robinson." This post derived its name from the fact that Lieutenant Robinson had been killed by the Indians near Fort Laramie three years prior to this. (As a coincident, I myself while a teamster at Fort Laramie, drove the ambulance that hauled Lieutenant Robinson's body into Fort Laramie, and I also drove the six-mule team that hauled the first load of commissaries to Camp Robinson). After establishing this camp, we returned to Fort Laramie, leaving about one-half of the command at Camp Robinson. Upon our arrival there, orders were awaiting Crook to select, from our six-mule teams, mules suitable for packing purposes, and with his command to report to Fort Fetterman. This was the first move directly of the Sioux War of 1876. There was also at Fort Laramie orders to organize what was called the Black Hills or Jenny expedition. Colonel Dodge was in charge of the military department and Professor Jenny was the scientist. The latter had instructions under military escort to enter the Black Hills and have it prospected for gold, as there had been rumors that miners from the north had gotten in there and found gold plentiful. This was then called the Popsy Paw country and was owned by the Sioux under treaties with the government. If Professor Jenny could verify this fact, the government's intention was to buy it from the Sioux. This would allow white men to go in there undisturbed.

I joined this expedition in the capacity of a teamster. I drove what was termed "Headquarter Wagon." This wagon contained the equipment belonging to General Dodge, and was always in the lead and thus termed the "Lead Wagon." Among teamsters, this was quite an honor and also quite a convenience, as one arrived in camp earlier than the many teams strung out in the rear.

The government was short of transportation and in addition to fifty government six-mule teams, they were compelled to hire forty teams owned by citizens, making in all ninety teams.

Before leaving Fort Laramie, I met up at the Sutler store a man named Botsford. He was an old government employe and when I first went to Cheyenne, he was superintendent of transportation for the government at a station close by, named Camp Carlin. All supplies destined for northern posts passed through his station, same having been brought there by the Union Pacific railroad. The superintendent was considered a very high official, having a great responsibility upon his hands. Botsford was a highly educated man and when off duty hobnobbed a good deal with the officers at Fort D. A. Russell, a short distance away. He was also very sporty and particularly fond of horse racing. At a horse race one day, he and Lieutenant Whiting had a serious misunderstand regarding some bet that was made. After the race Botsford went to Camp Carlin and later Lieutenant Whiting followed him there, when they got into a quarrel, Lieutenant Whiting drawing a sixshooter, shooting twice at Botsford, but missing him. Botsford being unarmed, ran to his quarters, the lieutenant following him. On a table lay Botsford's gun. He snatched it up, shooting the Lieutenant and killing him. This, of course, was a very serious matter—the killing of a United States officer.

About this time an ambulance drove up. Botsford jumped into it, ordering the driver to drive him to Cheyenne. He there gave himself up to the sheriff. Later, when the soldiers heard of the death of their lieutenant, they armed themselves and a great number of them started for Cheyenne to avenge the lieutenant's death. The citizens of Cheyenne, knowing that there would be serious trouble over the matter, also armed themselves and barricaded the streets leading up to the jail where Botsford was confined. This stopped the advance of the soldiers. Finally, officers from Fort D. A. Russell rode into Cheyenne and ordered the soldiers back to their quarters. Botsford later on was tried and acquitted, but naturally was discharged from the government's employ. He then began to carouse and drink heavily, and in six months he was a perfect sot. In fact, so low that he became a saloon bum.

In meeting at the sutler's store as previously stated, I said to him, "Why don't you brace up and come out with us on this expedition?"

He replied, "No; I am too far gone, and if I got away from whiskey for two days, I would die."

I then said to him, "Botsford, if you will agree to come along, I'll see Jim Duncan, the wagonmaster, and get you a position driving a six-mule team, and furthermore, I'll take whiskey enough along to brace you up. In doing this you can make a man of yourself again. You are too good a man to go on in the manner you are and here is your last chance."

The poor fellow began to cry and between sobs told me that those were the first encouraging words he had had spoken to him in two years. I left him and went down to the corral to see Duncan. I asked Duncan to give Botsford a chance. He laughed at me, saying that Botsford would not live three days.

I then told him my plan to brace Botsford up and also told him that three years prior to this, Botsford had done him many favors and that now was the time to reciprocate. However, Duncan replied, "Your heart is much larger than your head, and if you will attend to him, I'll give him a job." The next morning I had Botsford astride of the wheeler in a six-mule team.

In a few days the expedition started, and about six times a day I would go back to Botsford and give him a good, stiff drink of whiskey. I did not let many days go by before reducing both quantity and quality, and in two weeks one would not have recognized the Botsford of former days. An army officer who chanced to see Botsford driving his team, reported the fact to Colonel Dodge, telling him of Botsford's previous trouble with Lieutenant Whiting. This, of course, caused a great deal of talk among the officers and soldiers. Professor Jenny finally hearing of it, came over one night to Duncan's tent and asked him who this Botsford was. I was standing close by and Duncan called me, telling Professor Jenny at the same time that I could tell him all about the Botsford affair. Jenny invited me over to his tent and I gave him Botsford's past history. When I got through, he said that he wanted a private secretary and asked me if I thought Botsford would accept the position. I replied, "Yes, I'll see that he does accept it." I then hunted Botsford up and explained matters to him. He threw up his hands and said "No, and for God's sake let me alone where I am." Talking with him further, I discovered his reason for not wanting to accept the position. He explained that if he accepted the position it would throw him into the society of the officers which might lead to trouble for him. I then took him over to Jenny, leaving him there. In about two hours he came over to my tent and told me he had accepted the position. Botsford held this appointment for a long time and was very satisfactory to Professor Jenny. I will write more of this man later.

Another man of prominence who accompanied this expedition was a Mr. McGillacuty. Mr. McGillacuty had a national reputation and had surveyed the boundary line between British Columbia and the United States, His duties were to take the topography of the country.

Our guide on this expedition was California Joe, a very noted man in the west. This man was one of the greatest mountaineers the west ever produced, not excepting Freemont. I will also speak more of this great man later on.

In due time we arrived at the outskirts of the Black Hills, and made our first permanent camp on French Creek. The town of Custer City is now located there, named in honor of General Custer.

CHAPTER XVIII.

GOOD AND BAD ARMY OFFICIALS OF THIS EXPEDITION
— A TRIBUTE TO CAPTAIN BURKE — HOW HE
FOUGHT ONE OF HIS PRIVATES—FAIR AND SQUARE
—A TEAMSTER'S MANY TROUBLES—HOW A LIEU-
TENANT GOT EVEN—CALAMITY JANE.

AFTER we had formed this permanent camp,
Jenny and his assistants, who were miners and
citizens, he being allowed five of them, went
prospecting. In two weeks they found gold
on this creek in paying quantities. They
then went over the divide to Spring Creek, which
was but a few miles from their camp. They also
found gold there. It then became necessary
to send twenty-five teams back to Fort Laramie for
supplies. I was detailed as one of the twenty-five.
This trip was under the command of Captain Burke.
He was stationed at Fort Laramie when I arrived
there and during my stay. Officers of these frontier
posts favored, if possible, the teams and teamsters
that were stationed in their posts. Captain Burke had
risen from the ranks and was universally liked by all
who knew him, especially the citizens. In the army
at this time officers graduating from West Point
usually looked down on officers who had risen from
the ranks, but not so in Captain Burke's case, as he
was a very square and just man. I will cite you one
instance of his character as a man.

Some two years prior to this time at Fort Laramie,
the first sergeant of Burke's company, I, of the 14th
infantry, reported to him that he had a very troublesome, fighting soldier in the company, and who had
whipped in a fist fight two or three of his men and
who bragged that he could whip any man in Fort
Laramie in a rough and tumble fight. Burke told the

sergeant that at guard mount next day to march the
company down to the banks of the Platte Rver, about
a quarter of a mile east of the parade grounds. To
do this, they had to march by the teamsters' quarters
at the corral. The next day we teamsters, seeing the
company march by, wondered where they were going.
Suddenly they halted, and I and three others ran
down there to see what they were doing. Just as
we arrived, Burke had ordered this man, whose name
was Murphy, to advance five paces in front of the
company. The soldier did so. Burke then addressed
him as follows:

"My good man, my first sergeant informs me that
you have been making a great deal of trouble in the
company by fighting with and bullying your companions. He also states that you have made a boast
that you can whip, in a rough and tumble fight, any
man in Fort Laramie, and I am here to inform you
that there is one man in Fort Laramie who doubts
your ability to fulfill your boast, and that man is I."

The soldier replied: "You forget that you are a
captain and I a private, and that I dare not fight you."

Burke leisurely unbuttoned his coat, removing it,
and throwing it on the grass between himself and the
soldier, remarked: "There lies Captain Burke and
here stands plain, ordinary Dan Burke. Now prepare
yourself by removing your blouse and hat, for you are
going to have the time of your life." The soldier did
so, and at it they went; first one having the best of it,
and then the other.

They fought over the grass, rolling over and over;
sometimes Burke on top, other times the soldier. Blood
flowed freely. Finally, Burke got him by the throat
with his left hand, he being on top, then pressing his
knee against his abdomen, in the meantime choking
and punching him in the face, until the soldier shouted,
"enough." Burke arose, walked over to where his coat

and cap were; the soldier being unable to rise, two or three men stepped forward and helped him to his feet, and I assure you he was a sight. Burke was also very much disfigured. Captain Burke facing the soldier, then said: "Now go back to your quarters and behave yourself and always remember that there is one man at this post you cannot whip." He then marched the company back to their quarters, and in the future this soldier was a "good dog."

The news of this fight soon spread around the country, and I assure you that Burke raised a great many notches in the estimation of all who knew him.

We arrived at Fort Laramie in due time, nothing of particular interest occurring on the trip. We remained in Fort Laramie about a week, having our harnesses repaired, mules shod and wagons loaded. One beautiful morning orders were given for us to return to Jenny's camp, Burke still being in command.

At this time a lieutenant arrived at Fort Laramie from Arizona. His name was Ray. He had served under General Crook in the Apache War. He was a "West Pointer"—as we termed those who had graduated there—and had a very exalted opinion of himself, and hated a citizen and especially a teamster. He was appointed quartermaster on this return trip. To have the reader understand the authority invested in a quartermaster, I must explain that they have entire charge of the transportation and are held responsible to the commanding officer for anything occurring. The first day out this quartermaster began abusing the teamsters for any trifling thing they might do, and was very profane in his remarks, often calling them very vile names. We teamsters knew we had struck a tartar and tried our best to keep out of trouble with him.

About the third day out this fellow issued an order to the effect that all teamsters, after unhitching

their mules, after arrival in camp, should put their
halters on them and lead them fifty paces from the
camp. His reason for doing this was that the mules,
in being turned loose at the wagon, might stumble
against the guy ropes of the officers' tents and annoy
them. When unharnessing the mules, as soon as the
teamster has released the hames from the collars,
unbuckled the belly bands and unbuckled the collar,
the mules are gone with half the harness, if the
teamster is not very quick. The mules to some extent
are trained this way and to break them in to waiting
until they were completely unharnessed would be a
difficult job, as they were always very anxious to get
out to feed, since we did not carry feed for them on
these expeditions, not having room; the mules living
entirely on grass. As soon as they were released,
two or three teamsters were detailed each day to
herd them. Consequently, we paid no attention to the
order. The quartermaster did not notice this for a
couple of days.

We had a teamster in the outfit named Phillips.
He was a Missourian; very long and gangling, and the
butt of all our jokes. The quartermaster happened to
come along when Phillips was unhitching. He drove
four mules attached to an ambulance. He had just
turned two of his mules loose, when Ray called him
a vile name, saying, "Don't you know that I issued
an order that you d—— teamsters were to halter and
lead your mules fifty paces out of camp?"

Phillips did not answer him but proceeded to
unharness another mule. The quartermaster rushed
up to him and kicked him. Quicker than lightning,
Phillips shot out that great, large fist of his, hitting
the quartermaster between the eyes, knocking him
down. Ray had a six-shooter in a scabbard, which was
covered by a flap and buttoned, the same being attached to his belt. Reaching around he attempted to

unbutton this flap to draw his six-shooter. Phillips rushed to the front box of the ambulance where he carried his gun, getting it and throwing it down on Ray, telling him not to draw that six-shooter or he would kill him.

Ray exclaimed, "Don't shoot, teamster, don't shoot." Then, getting up, walked away, Phillips resuming the unhitching.

In about thirty minutes a corporal and three men put Phillips under arrest, and escorted him up to Captain Burke's tent, where Ray had already gone. The first question Burke asked the teamster was, "In what post are you employed?"

He replied, "Fort Laramie."

Burke then said, "The quartermaster informs me that you disobeyed his orders and also struck him. Is this a fact?"

Phillips replied, "Yes, sir."

"Why did you do so?"

Phillips then explained to Captain Burke the whole circumstances, also telling him that it would be almost impossible for a teamster to obey this order, and that he was very sorry it led up to any trouble. Burke then turned to the quartermaster, saying, "Lieutenant, I think you are too severe on our teamsters. This mode of treatment of them might do in Arizona but not in this country, and unless you change your ways, some of these Fort Laramie teamsters will severely injure you, for I know many of them and they are a hard set."

This was a good lesson to Ray and before the expedition was over we had very little trouble getting along with him.

With this same expedition was another young lieutenant; I can't remember his name, but he had recently arrived from West Point. One day, my team being in the lead, I saw sitting on the prairie by the side of a river, Captain Burke and three officers. Burke motioned me to drive in toward them. Then I knew we were going to camp there for the night. When I got up to where they were, I said, "Captain, where do you want this wagon to stand?"

He replied, "Unhitch where you are, teamster."

I had unhitched four of the mules, when this blustering, little lieutenant came along, and in a loud voice asked me why I was unhitching there. I told him, by orders of Captain Burke. He fumed around, finally ordering me to pull the wagon up ten paces further. I paid no attention to him and kept on unhitching the other team of mules. I thought the fellow would go crazy. Finally a mild voice said, "Lieutenant, what seems to be the trouble with you and that gentleman?" with emphasis on the gentleman, for it was very, very seldom a teamster was called a gentleman by an army officer.

However, the lieutenant saluted and replied, "I wish this wagon moved ten paces."

Burke then said: "No, no, lieutenant, I ordered the gentleman to unhitch there." I will ask the reader how could any teamster dislike this Captain Burke.

I had been around government long enough to know that this lieutenant, if he stayed with the expedition long enough, and having it in for me, would make it unpleasant for me if the opportunity presented itself, and sure enough it was but a few days before he supposedly got his revenge.

The quartermaster had issued an order that all teamsters should continuously ride their near saddle mule while in motion. On all government wagons teamsters would construct what we called . a lazy board. ˊ This was pushed under the wagon-bed between the fore and hind wheels on the near or left-hand side of the wagon, and when we got tired riding the saddle mule, we would pull out this lazy board and sit on it. This order was just, as a teamster sitting on the lazy board could not see all of his team. However, I was sitting on this lazy board when along came my friend, the lieutenant, and said, "Get up on that saddle mule." I did so. He rode by my side, he being mounted, for a half hour in hopes that I might say something to him, but not one word from me. When we arrived in camp and unhitched, a corporal walked down to our mess and informed me that the commanding officer wanted to see me. I went up there, and found, standing in the tent, the lieutenant. Captain Burke informed me that the lieutenant had reported me for disobeying orders by riding on my lazy board. I admitted the fact. Burke then turned to the lieutenant and said: "I am going to give this teamster a very severe sentence." This rather startled me. However, turning to me, Captain Burke said: "Teamster, go down to your mess, get an axe and immediately destroy that lazy board. After you have done so, bring the pieces and lay them at the door of this lieutenant's tent." I thanked him and backed out of the tent. I have no recollection of that lazy board being destroyed by me.

In due time we arrived at Jenny Camp and found that Professor Jenny had satisfied himself that gold was in paying quantities in that portion of the Black Hills. I will here mention why this portion of the country was called the Black Hills. On the outskirts of these hills and visible from the plains were a great many pine trees, very black, but upon getting close to them, they were a pronounced dark green. Thus the name "Black Hills."

It was from here that Professor Jenny and Professor McGillacuty sent their first report to the authorities in Washington. This report was transported by carrier to Fort Laramie and from there mailed to Washington. We remained in camp there awaiting orders, which came after the authorities had received this report. They ordered Jenny to further explore these hills. This order was imparted to Colonel Dodge and in three days we were again on the move.

As mentioned previously, I stated that California Joe was our guide. To give the reader some idea of the task that this man was attempting in an unknown country, I will explain that there were one hundred six-mule teams and ten companies of soldiers, part of which were cavalry. The mules and cavalry horses had to have grass and water to subsist on. The men also had to have water, and the commissaries that sustained these men, had to be transported with them. Bear in mind that there were no roads in this country and suitable ground had to be selected by the guide in order that the teams and soldiers could get through. Not once on the whole trip did this man make a mistake, and never one dry camp did we have to make.

After entering the hills, California Joe traveled entirely on foot, accompanied by a large black hound. Wearing an old cavalry overcoat, cavalry pants tucked in his boot tops, his gun in hand, and on his head an old black, broad-brimmed slouch hat, he would start out about the break of day, and before the command was ready to move, Joe would ascend to a hilltop and with his hands shading his eyes, would scan the country in all directions. He would then return to camp and report to Colonel Dodge, telling him the direction he wanted the teams to travel that day and that at times he would intercept us, if he wanted the route changed. This much accomplished, California Joe would then fill a buckskin sack with food enough to last twenty-four hours for both himself and the dog, carrying the sack himself.

We usually followed the ridges, sometimes descending to the river bed, and a few times it would be necessary to rough-lock with chains, the wagon wheels, and with a rope attached to the hind axle, then taking a turn with the rope around a tree; in this way securing the wagon, as otherwise it would have been impossible to have gotten down to the river bed. We never, at any time, turned back. Joe would appear on an average of twice a day to see how we were getting along.

▾ I remember one afternoon, after having had a pretty hard time of it all the morning, Colonel Dodge stopped the command to rest, when Joe happened to come along. Being driver of the headquarter wagon, I was always close to Colonel Dodge and his officers, and overheard Dodge ask Joe where we were going to camp that night.

Joe replied, "Colonel, do you see those two mountains off to the west? There we will find the headwaters of some river."

"How do you know this, Joe? You say you have never been in here before."

All the reply Joe would make was: "I can tell by the lay of the country."

Dodge smiled and said: "Joe, where is due north and south?"

Immediately Joe broke off a piece of dry grass and holding it between his thumb and finger, said: "Colonel, take out your store compass and if this piece is not pointing due north, I will eat my old hat."

Sure enough it was. The colonel looked at Joe a moment, and then said: "Joe, I would follow you through the wilds of Africa."

"Well," said Joe, shrugging his shoulders, "I could take you and the outfit through there."

To which Dodge replied: "I believe you." Then turning to the bugler, he ordered him to blow the march. We then moved on and in three hours we found the headwaters of Red River, and a beautiful spot it was. Surrounding it was a small, open valley, with plenty of grass, and to the astonishment of Professor Jenny, he found timothy hay growing there three feet high. How the seed ever got there was always a mystery.

Poor Joe was killed in 1878 by a teamster named Graham. They had been imbibing pretty freely at Cuney & Coffee's ranch, six miles above Fort Laramie on the Laramie River, and got into a dispute regarding our trip through the Black Hills, Graham having been a teamster at the time. They finally agreed to go out back of this ranch, put their backs together and walk fifteen steps in opposite directions, then turn and fire. Graham's nerve deserting him, friends interfered and stopped the quarrel. About two months later some teams were camped near Red Cloud Agency, Graham being one of the teamsters. Joe, who was living in that section of the country and seeing the teams camped, walked toward them; Graham seeing him, seized his gun and resting it on the wagon wheel, shot poor old Joe, killing him instantly. Graham immediately took to the hills, but was followed by a posse and captured three days later and was hanged to a tree. Thus ended one of the greatest mountaineers the west ever produced, and also ended the career of a black-hearted murderer.

Professor Jenny prospected these hills thoroughly. We often made camp and remained there for ten or fifteen days while he was doing so. Finally we got through the hills, coming out on the northwest side to the plains. We then skirted the hills on the north and east side on our way back to Fort Laramie, from where we had been gone five months.

The day before we arrived at Fort Laramie, my friend Botsford rode up to me and said, "Young, I don't know how to thank you for all you have done for me. This has been a glorious trip through a wonderful country and never in my life have I felt better and never in my life have I thought more of myself. With your assistance I have fought the fight of my life, and some day in the near future I will repay you ten-fold for what you have done for me." Taking me by the hand, he bowed his head and cried like a child.

I said to him, "Botsford, when we arrive at the post, don't forget that there is a sutler store there and in that sutler store they sell vile whiskey."

He replied, "Don't fear! never again! California Joe and I, when we receive our pay, are going to fit ourselves out and go back into the hills. I have selected a place there, and if it comes up to my expectation, you, Joe and myself, will have all the money we want for the balance of our lives. You need not come back with us, but if successful, I will find you if you are on earth." They remained at Laramie for only five days, then returning to the hills. I will explain to the readers later on how this man kept his word.

At this time, the true story of Calamity Jane's history will not be amiss. She was born at Fort Laramie in 1860. She was the daughter of a soldier named Dalton. Dalton was discharged from the army in 1861, and with his wife and daughter settled on a hay ranch on a stream called the La Bontie, 120 miles from Fort Laramie. In the early fall of that year a large body of Sioux Indians raided that country, kill-

ing all white persons that happened in their path.
Among those killed was Dalton. Mrs. Dalton was shot
in the eye with an arrow, destroying the sight, and
with her own hand extracted the arrow and quickly
bandaging the eye, placed her one-year old daughter
on her back and managed to escape. Traveling nights
and hiding by day, subsisting on weeds and roots, she
finally managed to reach Fort Laramie in eight days,
a mere skeleton of her former self, her clothing torn
to shreds. Before medical aid could be procured, she
expired. Sergeant Bassett, of company I, 14th infantry, and his wife adopted the child and prefixed to
her name, Jane Dalton, the word "Calamity," so hence-
forth she was known as Calamity Jane. She was the
pet of the fort and lived there until the spring of
1875. Jane was then about fifteen years of age, quite
good looking, dark complexioned, black eyes and black
hair, which she wore short. She had no particular use
for a citizen, but anybody with a blue coat and brass
buttons, could catch Calamity.

At this time Calamity Jane was enamored with
Sergeant Shaw, of company E, 3rd cavalry. His company having been detailed on the Jenny expedition,
and she wanting to accompany him, he suggested that
she wear cavalry clothes. He then secretly took her
to the company's tailor and fitted her out with a complete uniform. One not knowing her would never have
taken her for a female. She spent her time entirely
with this company and up to the time that we reached
our first permanent camp, none but Shaw, and possibly a few other soldiers, knew that she was with the
expedition.

In constructing this first permanent camp, they
arranged the officers' tents in a square, covering them
with bows cut from trees. This left a large space
which was termed the parade ground. One of the
tents was used as a sutler store, where was sold

whiskey, tobacco, etc. One morning Calamity had occasion to cross this square. Unfortunately, she met an officer, who was a German and a great disciplinarian, and having no chance to get by him, saluted him in true soldierly style. He saluted in return. Quite a number of officers were standing in front of the sutler tent, one of them knowing Calamity and seeing an opportunity for a joke on this officer, when the latter approached them he laughed at him. He asked him what he was laughing at. He made no reply, but laughed louder. The officer then demanded to know why they were laughing at him. They finally told him that the soldier he had just saluted was Calamity Jane. His dignity was hurt and he immediately made an investigation and found that it was true, and also found that Calamity was consorting with 1st-officer Shaw, which caused Shaw to be severely reprimanded, and also had an order issued expelling Calamity from the camp. Poor Calamity was in a quandary what to do. She could not go back to Fort Laramie alone, as the Indians were bad, etc.

As a final resort, Calamity Jane came up on the hill to where we teamsters were camped, and knowing me well, asked if she could go along with us. If so, she would do the cooking for our mess. I finally got permission from the wagonmaster to allow her to travel and camp with us. This compelled her to change her soldiers' clothes for citizen clothes, which we furnished her. She remained with us the balance of the way and naturally I saw much of her. When we moved camp, Calamity rode in my wagon whenever she got tired of walking.

One day when crossing Spring Creek, my wagon turned over as I was making a turn, which threw the rear end of the wagon into quite deep water. Calamity being under the wagon sheet, was compelled to crawl out of the hind end, and in doing so, fell into the water up to her neck. My! how she did swear at me; and she always seemed to have the idea that I did it purposely, but such was not the case, as it was considered a disgrace for a teamster to capsize his wagon and was also a great trouble to him. This girl became a very notorious character and I will later on speak of her further.

Before arriving at the Platte River, where Fort Laramie was situated, there was a high divide and when my team reached the pinacle of this divide, which gave them a view of the post and three very large hay stacks, they were about half starved and very, very thin and were also very much skinned up by the friction of the harness which they wore. Consequently, when my lead team saw this post, they began to bray, the balance of the hundred teams taking it up, making a horrible noise which was deafening. We had made this trip by long, severe drives and had not given the mules much chance to graze. However, the poor animals were now in sight of something good to eat, which accounted for the deafening noise they made.

On arriving at the river, we found a rudely constructed ferry boat or raft. This would only carry one team at a time. It being now about four o'clock in the afternoon, and by using this ferry, it would have taken all night to have ferried us across. The river in the channel for about fifty feet was deep enough to compel a team to swim. The wagons were about empty, as all the commissaries were about used up. I suggested to the wagonmaster, Jim Duncan, that we swim the outfit over. After some talk he consented to do so. Being mounted on a sorrel mule, he waded out in the river to the edge of the channel, with a whip in his hand, and, as we drove out to where he stood, he headed the teams upstream. This was a wonderful and exciting experience, as some mules were good swimmers; others would not swim, but as the channel was not wide, by the time the wheelers were compelled to swim, the leaders were far enough across to touch the bottom.

We succeeded in crossing the outfit in about two hours without losing a mule or having any serious accident. Jim then corraled the outfit, the mules braying all the time, when suddenly there loomed up, coming from the post, two large loads of hay. At the sight of this hay, the starved mules became almost unmanageable, jumping over the wagon tongue to which they were tied three on a side, getting tangled up in their halter shanks; some breaking away from the tongue and running toward the loads of hay, tearing into it, grasping great mouthfuls and devouring it. After feeding the teams, giving them all they could eat, two more wagons arrived loaded with sacks of oats. We then attached our feed box to the wagon tongue and fed them all they could eat. We remained in this camp for five days, and it is wonderful how these mules picked up flesh and, mule-like, they would kick one's head off if he were not very careful while wandering among them. Such is mule gratitude.

I have mentioned a great deal the expression "six-mule team" and for the benefit of the readers, I will describe a six-mule team, then in use by the government.

Starting in at the wagon, the two mules hitched, one on each side of the tongue, were termed wheelers or wheel-mules. Attached to the end of this tongue was what was termed a gooseneck, and attached to this gooseneck was what were called spreaders, which consisted of a straight bar, and on each end of this bar were single-trees, and to these were attached what was called the swing team. Also from the end of this tongue was attached a chain about twelve feet long, called a fifth chain, running between the swing mules. Suspended from the inside hame of each swing-mule was a small chain with a ring in the center, through which the fifth chain ran. This appliance was to keep the chain from sagging on the ground. To the end of this chain was another pair of spreaders, lighter in construction than the one at the end of the tongue, and to this was attached the lead mules. To the near lead mule or left-hand mule, from a small chain suspended from the lower part of the bit of the bridle was attached a strap made of leather about an inch and a half wide on that end, increasing in width and reaching back to the wheel-mule. This was called a lead line. The driver of the team sat in a saddle on the near wheel-mule, holding this strap in his hand when guiding the team. To the outer hame of the outside lead-mule was attached what was known as a jockey stick, which was about the size of a broom-stick. The opposite end of this stick was attached to the bit of the off-lead mule or the right-hand one. If one wanted the team to go to the right or gee, as it was called, the teamster jerked his lead line, and the near lead-mule, having been previously broken, would immediately turn to the right, forcing its mate to go likewise. If the teamster wanted to turn haw or to the left, he pulled on the lead line and they immediately turned. The traces used in those days were made of chain, covered with leather, which was called piping. This piping would become worn and the consequences would be that the bare chain would skin the mule up awfully, and I believe that this is why they termed teamsters "mule-skinners."

In those days there were no brakes on a government wagon, and if we wanted to stop our team, we had to depend entirely upon the wheelers to do so. They were also broken mules and at the word "whoa,"

they would sit back in their breeching, spreading out
from the tongue and with a chain, which was attached
from the end of the tongue to their hames, they would
hold back for dear life, and it is astonishing to me
now how they ever did it. In going down very steep
hills, we used a lock chain, which was attached to
each side of the wagon near the hind wheels, and loop-
ing this to the rim of the wheel behind a spoke, we
would attach it with a hook and a small ring fitting
over the end of the hook. This made the wheels
stationary. Again, in going down very steep hills, we
used a larger chain, which was called rough-locking.
With the free end of this, we took two or three turns
around the rim of the wheel, then making it fast,
allowed it to drag on the ground under the wheels;
thus the term "rough-locking."

CHAPTER XIX.

JIM DUNCAN, THE GREAT WAGONMASTER — CAMP
STAMBO IN THE SHOSHONE INDIAN COUNTRY—
TRANSFERRING CAVALRY COMPANIES—BACK TO
FORT STEELE AND FORT SAUNDERS—MY ONLY
EXPERIENCE AS A WAGONMASTER — PARKING
WOOD IN THE MOUNTAINS NEAR FORT FETTER-
MAN—ATTACKED BY THE INDIANS, WHO KILLED
MY PARTNER, MACK, THE WOOD-CHOPPER.

JIM DUNCAN was one of the oldest of old-time
wagonmasters in the west in those days. He
had driven a spike team in the Mexican War.
He had also acted as wagonmaster during our
rebellion and after that unpleasant affair he,
like hundreds of others, drifted to the far west. Jim
stood almost seven feet; very raw boned in physique,
long arms and legs, with very large hands and feet,
a steel gray eye, which was very piercing when he
looked at one, and a man absolutely fearless. His face
was considerably scarred up, for in his young days
he had participated in many broils, though not of his
own seeking. He dressed entirely in soldiers clothes,
wearing high topped boots, pants tucked in at the
top. In cold weather he wore a cavalry coat and
a black slouched hat, and I assure you he was the
picture of manhood and one of the most kind-hearted
men I ever had the pleasure of meeting. He admitted
to me one day that he was eighty-five years of age.

Jim Duncan was a great smoker and one scarcely
ever saw him without his little briarwood pipe in his
mouth. This pipe he would light, draw on it two or
three times, then forget to draw and let it go out.
He carried with him a pocketful of matches and was
continually relighting his pipe. This amused us
teamsters very much and I kept tab on him one day

and in one-half hour he had lighted his pipe twenty times, each time saying, "D—— this pipe; I can't seem to keep it lighted, and when I get time, I'm going to clean the d—— thing from mouth-piece to bowl," but I am quite sure that pipe was never cleaned.

It was said of Jim that he had worked so long for the government that he could not sleep unless the odor of a mule permeated the air. His feet being so large, compelled him to have his boots made to order, and on going to bed at night, myself and two others occupying the same tent with him and sleeping side by side in our blankets, we noticed that he always put his boots under his head, same acting as a pillow. In getting up in the morning very early, the tent being dark, he would fumble around, extracting his right boot first. In pulling it on, he would use a great deal of profanity, damning his big feet and after a great deal of stamping around, would finally get his boots on. The left boot he had no trouble with. One night I suggested to one of the teamsters that we steal his right boot, which we did, secreting it under the blankets at the lower end of our bed. Jim got up in the morning as usual and taking the left boot, tried to put it on the right foot, and I assure you the air was blue in that tent. Finally he lit a candle, then discovering that he had the left boot, he woke us up, or thought he did, and demanded his other boot. We all helped him hunt for it, finally finding it. He took it in his hand and looking at it a moment, said: "Either that d—— boot or I am crazy, and I believe I am the crazy one." This caused a great deal of laughter.

I remember another time when many of us teamsters were in a variety show in Cheyenne, kept by a man named McDaniels, and on this occasion the audience (which was large) ran this show to suit themselves—taking possession of the stage, etc., and if an actor or actress, or both, did not do their turn to suit, the audience would not allow the curtain to be lowered and made them do it over again. Jim this night was behind the scenes, the curtain dropped and he started to cross the stage, when someone suddenly raised the curtain. This exposed him about the center of the stage. The audience yelled with delight, many of them rushing on the stage, catching Jim, compelled him to do a turn before they would release him. This he did, singing in a cracked voice, without an accompaniment, that old-time song, "Betsy from Pike." At the end of this song, he danced an old-time jig. We compelled him to do this act three times, when the old fellow was exhausted. This made the greatest hit that ever appeared in McDaniels' Theatre.

The Jenny expedition disbanded at Fort Laramie; soldiers and citizens being paid five months' wages. An order then came from the War Department to transfer Company M of the 2nd Cavalry to Camp Stambo, which was situated in the Wind River Valley in the Shoshone Indian country. From there we moved E of the 2nd Cavalry to Fort Saunders. With this transfer went twenty-five six-mule teams, I being one of the drivers and Duncan as wagonmaster. We started on the 30th of September and had a beautiful trip, arriving there in the early part of October.

In that country was a very large hot springs and old Duncan having rheumatism very badly, we prevailed upon him to remain there for a month in hopes it would cure him. After a great deal of persuasion he finally did so. Each teamster donated a share of their provisions, or rations, and gave to him. This left a vacancy for a wagonmaster. Personally, I did not want the position, as I was rather quick tempered in those days and could not get along with army officers. However, Duncan insisted on my taking the job, to which I finally consented. Then the old fellow began to warn me not to have any trouble with the officers and to take good care of the mules, for if anything happened it would reflect upon him, as he had recommended me. I promised him that I would do the best I could. We finally started for Fort Steele on the line of the Union Pacific railroad.

We had not left the post to exceed four hours when I had a misunderstanding with the first sergeant of the cavalry company. He was continually annoying the teamsters and finally turned on me. We were both mounted, I riding Duncan's saddle mule and he a cavalry horse. After a while I lost my temper, rushed at him; when he attempted to draw his six-shooter, I being quicker than he, struck him over the head with my gun, knocking him from the horse. The largest part of the company were away in advance of the teams. The soldiers ran to him, picking him up and dressing his wounds, tying a bandage around his head. The sergeant then mounted his horse and riding off, reported me to Captain Peal, telling him a lot of things that were not true.

When we made camp that evening, the lieutenant, who was acting as quartermaster, detailed a corporal and three men, instructing them to bring me to his tent. They found me up in the mess wagon and ordered me to come with them, which I refused to do. The corporal attempted to get up in the hind end of the wagon, when I told him that if he came any farther, I would kill him. By this time the teamsters had gathered around the wagon, telling me that they would stand by me. Hearing the commotion, the lieutenant came up, telling the corporal to get up in the wagon and take me out. I told the lieutenant that I knew soldiers had to obey orders and instead of getting this man injured, for him to come up and take me out. He immediately took me at my word, and as he arose to a standing position in the wagon, I tackled him, the teamsters holding the soldiers back so they could not injure me or assist the lieutenant. Presently I heard the words, "What is all this trouble about?" Looking up, I saw Captain Peal. He knew me, having been stationed at Fort Laramie previous to this. They separated us and, taking me by the arm, the Captain walked me down to his tent and the first thing he did was to give me a good, stiff drink of brandy; then saying, "Wagonmaster, I want you to tell me your side of the trouble with my 1st Sergeant." I did so, telling him the truth. He then said, " I am surprised at you, knowing that we must have discipline, and I fear that you have gotten into serious difficulties." He then gave me another drink, which was very acceptable under the circumstances; he, of course, each time joining me in the drink.

The captain then said, "I do not want to punish you severely, but I should order you in irons until we arrive at Fort Steele."

I replied, "Captain, I am a citizen, not a soldier, and am willing to quit my position and walk back to Camp Stambo, but I will not go in irons alive."

"Then the only way out of this trouble that I can see is to form the company in line and have you make a public apology to the lieutenant, as the sergeant seems to be satisfied in his part of the affair and has not made any charge against you." I told him no; that I could not even do that. Presently, in came the lieutenant. The captain again passed the liquor around. The lieutenant looking at both of us said, "Captain, this is a pretty husky wagonmaster we have."

He replied, "Yes, he is an old acquaintance of mine from Fort Laramie, and lieutenant, if this man apologizes to you here, are you willing to let the matter drop?"

The lieutenant replied, "Yes, sir. I will do better than that. After his apology, I will shake him by the hand, for it takes a pretty good man to handle me the way he did, and I was very glad that you appeared on the scene when you did, for I fear I would not have been able to have continued on the trip."

I made the apology and told him that I believed he was a good fellow after all. We then took another drink, and the matter ended there. The balance of the trip was very pleasant to all concerned. We finally arrived at Fort Steele, remained there a few days, then going down to Fort Saunders, situated near Laramie City, but now abandoned. There they turned the outfit over to me and I proceeded on to Camp Carlin, where I turned the teams over to the superintendent and was there paid my wages. The superintendent, Perry Organ, asked me to stay around there a few days and he would send me out as a wagonmaster with some teams going north. I thanked him, telling him that I had no more desire to be a wagonmaster. I remained there a few days until I got rid of my money in Cheyenne, from there going to Fort Fetterman.

Upon arriving at Fort Fetterman, I met my old friend, Jack Hunton. Jack informed me that I was the very man he was looking for. He had the wood contract for that year for the post and was short about fifty cords to complete the contract. The Indians were quite bad around there at that time and it was difficult to get a white man to go out in the mountains. He informed me that this wood was cut and piled on very steep side hills in the mountains twenty miles from there, and that he had arranged with one man named "Old Mack," the wood-chopper, but required

another to go with him. He offered me ten dollars per
day, furnishing a mule-team, wagon, guns, blankets
and provisions, if I would go, and help park this wood
—meaning by that, to haul it from side hills to where
they could get at it with ox teams to transport it to
the post. I told him it depended on the other man,
I not knowing him and wanting to know what kind of
a man he was. I was introduced to the other man,
and after talking with him for a time, found he was
all right. I then accepted the position. We started
out next morning, arriving at the spot about dark
and there we found an old log cabin, it having been
used by the wood choppers and there we made camp.

That night I talked the matter over thoroughly
with Mack, and we agreed to stay together, knowing
the Indians were bad, and, if separated at any time,
we were not under any circumstances to shoot a gun
off unless it were at an Indian. We took this precaution as game was very plentiful in these mountains.
We worked there for five days, I driving the team
and after the wagon was loaded, we rough-locked it
before starting down the steep hillside. Mack, walking on the offside of the wagon, carrying both of the
guns, I on the near side, driving the team, walking on
the ground, as it would be dangerous to ride on the
load in case anything should break.

On the sixth day, Mack conceived the idea of burn-
ing a charcoal pit, he having followed that occupation
and understood it, explaining to me that in this way
we could make some side money. I objected to this,
reminding him of our agreement and also telling him
that it was not treating Hunton right; that he had
employed us to park wood, not to burn charcoal pits.
However, he finally talked me into it and selected a
place inclosed by three rocky ridges, on the edge of
a deep, rough canyon through which flowed a stream,
named Box Elder. This stream emptied into the

Platte River, ten miles below there. The following
morning he started out with his axe in one hand and
gun in the other. We each carried forty-one rounds
of ammunition, forty of which were in a belt around
our bodies, the other in the gun. I put on a load of
wood, now being alone and started down the hillside.

On the opposite side of the wagon was a small
stump which I could not see. I ran against this with
the off forewheel. There was no way to get clear of
it except to unload the wagon. This, of course, made
me very angry at Mack. However, setting my gun
against the rear wagon wheel, I started to throw off
the wood and had thrown but a few sticks to the
ground, when I heard a gun shot coming from the
direction where Mack was. I quickly jumped to the
ground when I heard the second shot. Grasping my
gun, I ran up the hillside as fast as I could and when
within a few feet of the top, I saw two Indians dis-
appear over the ridge to the north. I knew then that
Mack was killed. In a few moments a shot was fired
from the opposite direction to where I saw the two
Indians. Having my right hand around the breech of
the gun near the trigger, the shot struck my finger,
breaking the gun at the breech. Looking over my
shoulder I saw three young bucks running toward
me, occasionally dodging behind a rock. I could not
shoot at them for my gun was out of commission and
I dare not let them know by any action of mine, that
such was the case. I knew my only chance was to
get down into Box Elder Canyon, where it was very,
very rough. Occasionally these fellows would take a
shot at me, but fortunately not hitting me, and when
they exposed themselves, I would point my gun at
them, when they immediately would dodge to cover.
I would then run farther down into the canyon,
finally getting to the bottom and not seeing any more
of my pursuers, I headed for the Platte River, crawl-

ing over and around great rocks and fallen trees. Darkness came on, but I still kept on going and tired and worn out I eventually reached the Platte River about daylight next morning. I then had open country to travel in and reached the post about one o'clock in the afternoon a sorrowful looking sight, my finger giving me a great deal of pain and all the time bleeding profusely. I had my finger attended to by the Post surgeon, to whom I reported the affair, then going to the commanding officer, reported it again to him. He looked at me a few moments, saying, "It serves you right. Why did you go out into the hills when you knew the Indians were bad around there?" I then asked him if he would give me an ambulance and a small escort of soldiers to go out and bring in the body. He then sent his orderly for some other officers and after some conversation, he furnished the escort, I going with them and riding in the ambulance.

We got started about four in the afternoon and traveling rapidly we arrived at a spring about two miles from where the body lay. The officers ordered a halt; I supposed for the purpose of watering the horses, but to my astonishment, they began unsaddling them. I asked the lieutenant in charge if he were going to camp. He replied, "Yes, as it would be dangerous to go into the hills at that hour of the night." I then told him that I was afraid the wolves would eat the body and asked him to detail two soldiers to accompany me and I would take care of the body until they arrived in the morning. He finally did so. One of the men detailed was a very excitable fellow. When we arrived in the hills, I had no trouble finding Mack's body. He was lying on his face with his left hand under his breast, his right hand extended, with two gun shots in his back, also an arrow which protruded about four inches. He was scalped completely, except for a little hair on the lower part of the head.

We built a fire close by the body, and lay down quite a distance from the fire. The exciteable man would imagine every few moments that he saw an Indian crawling up on us and wanted to shoot at him. We had great trouble in convincing him that there was no danger from Indians at that time. Daylight finally came, the ambulance and escort arriving, when we loaded poor old Mack's body in the ambulance and started back to Fort Fetterman, arriving there about eleven o'clock in the morning. We immediately buried Mack as the stench from the body was then very bad. This ended my wood parking business and I never learned whether the job was completed or not.

After the death of my partner, old Mac, I resumed my occupation of teamster at Fetterman, but only lasted one week. There were two cliques of officers at that post, and when they wanted to have a good time they would select Sunday. Ordering one six-mule team hitched up, and putting liquid refreshments in the wagon, they proceeded up the Platte River about five miles, and there had their time. It was an unwritten law in all posts that teamsters did not hitch up Sundays unless it was an absolute necessity. This day was set apart for teamsters to wash and mend their clothes, etc. I refused to hitch up when ordered by the wagonmaster. He reported me to the quartermaster. I was then put under arrest, and finally was escorted by a sergeant and four men to the edge of the post, tied face up on a brass cannon that was used to fire at sunset each night. There I remained for twenty minutes. The flies were very plentiful, and they swarmed on my face and hands, getting up my nostrels and into my eyes. After releasing me, I still stood pat and would not hitch up the team. I was then put in the guard house until midnight and in the morning discharged and escorted off the reservation. I walked to Fort Laramie, a blackballed teamster. The reader would naturally ask, why did you stand for this treatment? Simply because you could not help yourself, as government posts were far from towns, and if you wished to remain in the post and follow the business of teamster you had to stand for many things. The officers were supreme.

CHAPTER XX.

CUSTER CITY, THE FIRST TOWN ESTABLISHED IN THE
   BLACK HILLS—HEYDAY TIMES IN THE HILLS—
   PROVINCIAL GOVERNMENT.

ON the first day of November, 1875, there
came into Fort Laramie a Mr. Jones, Mart
Gibbons, Charley Smith, and another old
gentleman, whose name I can't recall. The
first two mentioned I knew on Red Cloud
Agency when I worked there. They had a four-
horse team loaded with supplies and in the load was
a barrel of high-proof whiskey. Jones was originally
from California, having kept merchandising stores at
various mining camps in that country. They were all
well armed and were going into the Black Hills. Jones
and Gibbons invited me to go with them. We started
and in due time arrived at Jenny's old camp on French
Creek. There we found quite a number of houses of
various size constructed of logs, some of which were
hewn, and living there were about a hundred men,
mostly miners. They were getting good pay from the
creek and as this looked good to us, we remained there.
Others came. The town grew rapidly and I finally
concluded to go into the saloon business in a small
way. Jones having this barrel of whiskey, I knew
I could get a starter there, but where to get the
glasses and other paraphernalia that would be necessary for a saloon, I did not know.

However, I rented one of the vacant buildings,
intending to start up with the whiskey alone. In a
few days a large outfit arrived there and among them
was an old friend of mine named Sam Gaylord, whom
I used to know in Dodge City, Kansas. He had a bar
outfit, intending to go into the saloon business. Gaylord having brought plenty of liquor with him of

various kinds and I having the location, we entered into a partnership and opened up the best equipped saloon that was ever conducted in Custer City.

After the town began to get established, the leading citizens called a meeting for the purpose of forming some kind of local government there and finally decided to have a provincial government. The next night they met again. These meetings were held in our saloon, which of course brought business to our bar. They then appointed a man named Farnum for Mayor; another by the name of Keiffer, was appointed Justice of the Peace; appointed another man as prosecuting attorney, whose name I forgot; John Burrows was made marshal. Burrows was from Denver, Colorado, and had been marshal there. He was quite large in stature and always wore two large six-shooters stuck in his belt. The appointment of marshal had been first offered to me, but I refused. Four days later the Mayor and Prosecuting Attorney concluded that Burrows should have a deputy, as the hours were too long for one man. They advised me to take this position and as it would make me more popular and would bring business to the saloon, I accepted, taking the watch from twelve noon until twelve midnight; Burrows taking the other shift.

In the meantime people were arriving in large numbers and it kept both Burrows and myself quite busy keeping order. The principle of this provincial government was, that if the law was broken in any way, we tried the offender in day light, subpoening a jury of twelve men and, if he had means, he had the privilege of employing an attorney or some one to defend him. If found guilty of a serious offense, we would send him to Cheyenne, where he could be tried in a recognized court of justice. If not serious, we always fined him in dollars and cents, this money being used to defray expenses of our government.

One afternoon while I was on duty, I was sitting in a barber's chair getting shaved. The barber had just lathered my face, when I heard a gun shot and in a few moments another shot. I snatched the towel from my neck and wiping off the lather, rushed out of the door, and saw a man lying on the ground and another man standing over him with a six-shooter in his hand. They were in front of a saloon about fifty yards away from where I stood; the saloon being situated on the bank of the creek. With others I ran down there and sneaking up behind the man who was standing, caught him around the arms pinning them to his side, and asked some one in the crowd to disarm him, which they did. I then hurried him into a vacant log cabin close by, closing the door and barring it and admitting only two others with me. We then found that the man who did the shooting was intoxicated and was very much excited. I told him to compose himself as I wanted to ask him some questions. He sat down on the floor and cried like a child, but finally controlling himself, when I asked him why he had killed the other man. He replied, "My God, is he dead? He is my partner and the best friend I ever had in the world." Further questioning him for his name and where he was from, he told me he was Tom Milligan and that he was from Eureka, Nevada. I then left him in charge of the other two men and, going out of doors, inquired of two or three persons who saw the shooting, how it occurred.

I learned from these men that Milligan and his partner staggered out of the saloon door, his partner telling Milligan to take a shot at an oaken bucket that we used in drawing water from a well, situated in the center of the town. Milligan did so. He then said, "Shoot again, Tom." As Tom did so, his partner staggered in front of him and the ball penetrated his head above the right eye, killing him instantly.

A very large crowd in the meantime had gathered around the cabin where I had him confined, and not knowing the particulars of the shooting, made threats that they wanted to hang him. I talked to them, telling them about our form of government there and that we would give him a trial the following day, and that they must not harm him. Some agreed to this, while others threatened what they would do. By this time it was getting dark and I entered the cabin and talked with Milligan. He told me he knew that he would be hanged that night. I replied, "If they hang you tonight, they will have to kill me first; and to show you I mean what I say, I will send one of these men up to my saloon and have him bring down here two guns, one a shotgun loaded with buckshot and the other a Winchester. You can take one and I the other and when it gets a little darker, I am going to take you down the creek to where I have a long cabin, and there you will be safer than you are here."

This surprised him very much and gave him great confidence in me. I then sent one of the men to my place. He procured the guns and brought them to me. I offered Milligan his choice and he took the Winchester.

Four or five of my friends wanted to assist me in protecting the prisoner, but I told them no, and that they could better protect him by mingling among the crowd, advising the crowd to wait until the morrow before they attempted any violence, and that I would assure them that they would change their minds when they heard the evidence. This they did. I then took Milligan down to the cabin mentioned, remaining there until nine o'clock the next morning.

When I brought the prisoner up to the building used for the courtroom, it was crowded. And there I discovered Milligan was a prominent Mason in good standing. Personally, I am not a Mason, but l could readily see in the actions of men whom I knew were, that Milligan would get a fair and square trial. About this time Burrows appeared on the scene and strutted around like a peacock, being very officious. I had sent the two men the night previous to find Burrows, but he could not be found. This convinced me that he was a coward, and I paid no attention to him. We gave Milligan his trial and the jury acquitted him, except that they fined him twenty-five dollars for shooting his gun off within the city limits.

The trial over, we buried Milligan's partner that afternoon. Milligan attended the funeral, I walking by his side, and never in my life have I seen a man so deeply affected. There were many in the town who still wished to hang him, and thinking they might injure him, I advised him to leave Custer that night. He told me he had no horse. I loaned him mine and he left about ten o'clock. I told him if he arrived at Fort Laramie safely to send the horse back to me by someone he could trust. Fortunately, when he arrived at Laramie, he met his brother Ed, who was also from Eureka, and of course told him about the manner in which I had treated him and about his trouble, turning the horse over to Ed, who arrived in Custer in due time, and we naturally became great friends.

I never knew what became of Tom after he reached Laramie, but poor Ed two years later, I heard, shot himself accidentally and died from the wounds in Sidney, Nebraska.

After this experience, I concluded I did not want any more of the "marshal business," and resigned the following day. This killing was the first white man killed by one of his own race in the Black Hills.

CHAPTER XXI.

ORGANIZING THE CUSTER CITY SCOUTS — CAPTAIN
JACK CRAWFORD, THE POST SCOUT—THE DEAD-
WOOD STAMPEDE—JIM WALL—A DYING CONFES-
FESSION FROM A MAN WHO DID NOT DIE.

REQUIRING more buildings in the town, quite
a number of men engaged in the occupation
of cutting and hauling logs suitable for that
purpose, the trees growing on a ridge about
two miles distant. While engaged in this
business the Sioux Indians killed two of the party,
and the men refused to continue work until the citizens called a meeting to discuss some means of protection for them. This the citizens did, the meeting
taking place in my saloon.

The evening of the meeting there arrived in the
town a man with long hair, broad-brimmed hat and
wearing a buckskin jacket. Hearing of the meeting,
he came down into the saloon and introduced himself
to me as Jack Crawford and said he was a correspondent for the Omaha Bee, and would like to report
this meeting. I introduced him to the mayor and two
others, who granted him the privilege sought. At
the meeting we concluded to appoint five men to act
as guards for the log cutters, and named them the
Custer City Scouts. Later in the evening Crawford
took me aside, saying, "Young, the principal part of
my business out here is to make a reputation, study
the habits of the country, and, if possible, to learn
something of the Sioux Indians." He also told me
that he was a poet, and in an off-hand way, quoted
some poetry of the Bret Harte style, which I considered very good. He then asked me if I could have
him appointed chief of our scouts. Having made a
good impression upon me, I told him I would talk with

the mayor, and I asked him to call on me next morning. The mayor and others took kindly to the proposition and the following day we appointed him the chief. We then notified the log cutters of what had taken place and they immediately resumed work under the guard appointed.

This was the means of bringing Crawford his first notoriety as a scout. He was a temperate man, neither drinking nor using tobacco; something very unusual in those days. He became very popular there and entertained us very often with his poems.

Crawford being out one day on a scouting trip alone, found lying in the grass, very sick, what he supposed to be a full-blooded Sioux Indian. Jack gave him some water, and seeing his chance to learn something of the Indian characteristics, secretly brought this sick man to his cabin after dark, and took care of him, not letting any of the citizens know, as he feared they might kill him. The Indian finally became so sick that he concluded he was going to die, and turning to Jack said in good English, "Go down and bring Young up here. I knew him at Fort Fetterman and know that he would like to talk with me."

I went to his cabin and was much surprised to find that the supposed Indian was Jules Seminole, a half-breed Sioux, but a renegade, and I knew that he was worse than any full-blood. He asked Crawford to step out of the room, as he wished to tell me something.

The reader will recall the shooting of my partner, old Mack, the wood-chopper, near Fetterman. Seminole told me that he was a brother-in-law of a man named Sneed Stagner, who was a squaw-man and took sub-contracts for cordwood for Fort Fetterman. Stagner owed old Mack three hundred dollars for chopping wood, and to cancel his debt, he gave Seminole one hundred dollars to kill old Mack. He also said it was he and another Indian I saw running over the point of the ridge and that I was lucky the other three Indians who were with him did not get my scalp. I was dumbfounded with his story. I thought the matter over and decided to wait and see if Seminole recovered. If so, I would then place him under arrest and take him to Cheyenne, where he would receive proper punishment.

My decision showed poor judgment, however, for two weeks later Seminole suddenly disappeared, taking with him Crawford's horse. I regretted then that I had not given him his just deserts. I learned later that he was hanged in South Dakota for murdering a sheep herder, and I hope the report is true. Years after this Crawford had shows out on the road, himself being leading man. Of course, his plays were of the Indian character, and I understand that he has made a great deal of money.

One day there arrived in Custer three four-horse teams, the wagons containing a large saloon outfit and fourteen dance-hall girls. They had come from Cheyenne and were brought in there by a man named Al Swarringer. Accompanying them were eight men who were gamblers. Their arrival created quite a commotion as we now knew we were going to have some amusement. Swarringer immediately constructed a large log building, flooring it, and in the rear erected fourteen stalls, or rooms, where the girls slept. At the back of the building was a shed in which they cooked and ate. This new enterprise took the town by storm and Swarringer made a great deal of money there. Among these girls was one named Georgia Dow, whom I had known in Hayes City, Kansas. Georgia was the queen of the dance-hall girls in Custer, she having been a long time in the business. She remained in that country until the fall of 1876, following her occupation, when she went to

Sydney, Nebraska, partially reforming, and I have been told she died at the age of 60. This is very remarkable, as that class of girls dissipated awfully and were frightfully abused by their lovers, who took from them all they could earn and frequently punished them severely when they did not earn enough. Georgia was a very kind-hearted girl and when anyone was sick or injured, she was the first to offer her assistance.

One afternoon there walked into my saloon my friend Botsford, of whom I have previously spoken. He quietly informed me that he had discovered rich diggings on a stream he had named Deadwood, which was seventy-five miles northwest from Custer. The name Deadwood was derived from the large amount of dead timber found along the stream. He exhibited two well-filled pokes or sacks of gold, and remarked that he had staked out a claim for me and that he had come in for supplies, intending to return in a few days. Botsford asked me not to mention this fact until he had gone, as it would cause a stampede, but to go there as soon as I could settle my affairs in Custer; adding, that if a stampede occurred, he would be unable to hold the claim for me unless I were present. In three days he left. On the fifth day the news in some way had leaked out about the discovery, but through what source I am unable to say. I do know, however, that I had not mentioned it to anyone—and such a stampede was never witnessed again in that country. The town was practically deserted in twenty-four hours.

My partner also got the fever, and without telling me, went to the corral and borrowed my horse, saddle and bridle. This left me a building and saloon fixtures on hand, but no customers. In about ten days I concluded to migrate to the new diggings, and, nailing up the doors and windows of the saloon, departed.

Arriving at Deadwood in due time, I found my claim was jumped. On going to Botsford and telling him of the fact, he said, "Don't worry. I have another one staked out for you on Whitewood." Whitewood was a branch of Deadwood. I worked this claim with four other men, but could not find the pay streak, and when my ready cash was gone, I abandoned it. Others took possession of it, but never found anything of value and it was known as a blank.

It being very difficult and expensive to get a location in the town of Deadwood, which was building up very rapidly, no one paid much attention to the location of his house. The gulch was very deep and narrow, and on the north side was a very high ridge consisting of great rocks, which made it impossible to build against the side hill. I finally concluded I would go to work. A man named Bill Nuttle had partly completed a large, hewed log building, and having expended all his money in doing so, was compelled to dispose of the building as it stood. Carl Mann and Jerry Lewis purchased it and completed it. Mann was a saloon man and Lewis a gambler,—one from Montana and the other from Nebraska.

These men named this saloon "Sixty-six." They employed me to attend to the bar. After opening they sent a wagon, drawn by a four-horse team, to Custer City to bring in my liquors that I had left there, intending to pay me for them. On arriving there they found the saloon broken open and everything of value gone. The "Sixty-six" saloon was one of the largest in that country at this time. We had in operation two faro games, a chuckaluck game and a twenty-one game. Poker and other short card games were also played. The town was booming, great numbers of people coming in each day from the north and the south. The diggings were shallow and rich, and a great deal of gold dust was taken out in a

short time. One of the most successful miners was
a man named Jack McAller, commonly called Black
Jack on account of his dark complexion and hair. This
fellow was looked upon as king of the town, but of
course, there were many lesser lights who were all
great money spenders, as pioneers of this sort usually
are. Swarringer had moved his dance-hall girls from
Custer, using a building opposite the saloon as a dance
hall.

The circulating medium of the town was gold dust.
If a greenback showed up, it was immediately put out
of circulation, as it was much easier to remit for supplies than gold dust. Every saloon and business house
had gold scales for weighing the dust, and I became
very expert at this business and had the reputation
at that time of being the quickest gold dust weigher
in Deadwood. In handling gold dust, and before
weighing it, we emptied it from the poke or sack into
a tin receptacle, the shape of a fire shovel minus the
handle, called a blower. We then ran through it a
steel magnet to learn if it were pure, as clean gold
was worth more per ounce than gold carrying iron or
other substances. If one wanted to take from it, say
fifty cents' worth, he pinched it between his thumb
and index finger, and with practice it was astonishing
how close to the amount desired could be pinched.
This was why I was called a fast weigher. It seemed
to come naturally to me and often miners would wager
money on my ability to pinch the amount designated.
Later on I purchased a square piece of Brussels carpet upon which I set the gold scales. This carpet
extended out from the scales about six inches on each
side, and in going from the receptacle to the scales,
by moving one's finger and thumb a little, one would
drop into this carpet quite a few particles of gold dust,
and it was very common to me, when going off watch,
to shake out eight or ten dollars' worth. This was

termed "side money," and was universally practiced in that town.

Our strongest competitors there were John Mann and John Manning. They owned the "Montana Saloon," same deriving its name from their native state. Another strong competitor was Jim Pencil, who was also from Montana. There were a few other smaller competitors. There were also some great characters in this town, who mostly had nicknames. First, "Johnny the Oyster," "Club Foot Frank," "Cheating Sheely," "Laughing Sam," "Pink Bedford," "Cliff Sane," "Frank Connelly," "Bloody Dick," and many others too numerous to mention.

In the late spring of 1876, I had occasion to make a trip by stage from Deadwood to Custer City. My companions consisted of a dance-hall girl, a Jew and four other men, one of whom everybody called "Telegraphy," he having constructed the telegraph line from Fort Laramie to Deadwood. The stage left Deadwood at ten o'clock P. M. About midnight we were dozing while the stage was slowly ascending a hill, the night not being very dark.

Presently the stage came to a sudden stop, awakening the occupants, when a loud voice commanded: "Hands up!" a shotgun pointing in one door and two six-shooters in the other. This same voice, accompanied by a great deal of profanity, ordered us to get out with our hands up and stand in line. This we did in a remarkably short space of time. It is surprising how quickly one can move and how long one can keep his hands up. The dance-hall girl became hysterical and screeched. They paid no attention to her. My position was in the middle of the line with a road agent standing at each end and one standing at the horses' heads, with his gun pointed at the driver. The fourth one, with his six-shooter in his left hand, performed the gentlemanly act of collecting

our toll. This man, having no disguise, I readily recognized him as an old teamster friend. We had driven
a team together for about two years. His name was
Jim Wall. My first thought was, "will he rob me?"
I had on my person five hundred dollars in greenbacks,
and at that particular time the loss of it would have
caused me considerable embarrassment. The Jew
begged piteously, asserting that he was dead broke,
and if they would not kill him, when he arrived in
Cheyenne he would send them five hundred dollars to
any place they might designate.

Wall laughed at the Jew and leisurely started feeling around his waist, and found a money belt (which
the Jew afterward claimed contained fifteen hundred
dollars). The Jew then collapsed, falling on the
ground as dead. Wall then went through his pockets,
relieving them of what small change they contained.
The next in line was Telegraphy. Wall, knowing him
and also knowing that Telegraphy was a hard whisky
drinker, remarked: "Telegraphy, you are not making
this trip without a bottle of whisky."

Telegraphy, in a clear voice, replied: "There is a
bottle under the cushion of the rear seat."

Wall ordered one of his men to get it, while he
himself went through Telegraphy's clothes as he had
done with the Jew's. Wall's confederate, handing him
the bottle, the former placed it at Telegraph's mouth
and said: "Sample it, I fear it may be doped."

Telegraphy, realizing that it would be his last
drink for some hours, grabbed the bottle with the intention of taking a large drink. Snatching the bottle
from his hand, Wall said: "Hands up, we will take
a chance at this." I assure the reader by this time it
was becoming very amusing to me, but still I could
not forget the thought—was I to lose my money!
Wall looked at me for a moment and playfully tapping

me under the chin with his six-shooter, remarked in a low tone, "I see, old pal, you are also caught in the net!" But he did not molest me. Passing on to the last two men, he quickly relieved them of their cash and valuables. He did not rob the girl. They then took the Wells-Fargo strong box, which seemed to be very heavy, and ordered us back into the stage, telling the driver to drive on and not look back for thirty minutes, bidding us "good night."

We then started. It was some time before the Jew could talk and the first thing he did was to feel in his boot legs, where was concealed five hundred dollars, which Wall had overlooked.

In a short time my troubles began. The four men openly charged me with standing in with the road agents, which was a natural supposition, as Wall had not robbed me. The Jew was the most pronounced in his remarks and I was forced to stop his talk. I then explained to the other men my previous acquaintance with Wall. Telegraphy believed me, and soon convinced the others. My destination being only to Custer City, on my getting out of the stage the Jew again became furious, saying that I was going back to meet the road agents and get my share of the spoils. I believe today, if he is alive, he is still of the same opinion.

Many times I have heard men discussing what they would do in case of being held up, but I can assure you, dear reader, that they would do exactly as we did by obeying the commands of the road agents.

Jim Wall was captured by the Pinkertons' agents two years after I left that country and was sentenced to Leavenworth Military Prison, having been tried on the charge of robbing the United States mail. His sentence was twenty-two years, and I understand he died three years after his incarceration.

CHAPTER XXII.

SIOUX INDIANS STEALING THE MONTANA HERD—
SCALPING AN INDIAN—CALAMITY JANE—A ROAD
AGENT—THE CUSTER MASSACRE.

THERE were a great many saddle horses in that country and feed being very high, it made it very expensive to keep them in town. Four young men conceived the idea of soliciting the owners of these saddle horses and agreeing for a certain sum of money per month, to herd them on the open plains near Crook City. They secured about two hundred of them and formed what was called the Montana herd. One Sunday a man came into Deadwood and in a very excited state told us that a large band of Sioux had run off the Montana herd, killing the four herders, the Indians having slipped up on them at daybreak.

This occurrence left very few horses in Deadwood. Those there were used principally for teaming purposes. However, we hurriedly formed a party, consisting of Carl Mann, Tom Dozier, Seith Bullock, Ed Milligan, Pat Kelly, John Varnes, Charley Storms, and a man named Brown, who had high aspirations to be appointed our first sheriff. These men, together with about twenty others, including myself, started on the Indian chase, who had gone to the north. Our horses were not very good saddle horses, as we had taken them out of the teams and livery stable. This placed us at a disadvantage. We followed the Indians for two days, not catching up with them. Our horses became jaded and we decided to return. Tom Dozier and I were riding side by side, considerably ahead of the balance, when I saw what appeared to be a large wolf, in the bottom of a dry creek. I called Tom's attention to it, remarking that if it were not for the noise made by our guns, it would be a fine shot. The words were hardly out of my mouth when the supposed wolf (but in reality an Indian, who had been on all fours digging with his hands in the creek bottom for water) rose up and started for some tall, dense plum bushes bordering the creek. We instantly gave chase and surrounded the spot where we knew he was concealed under a tree, the roots of which projected over the bank. We fired a great many shots but it was impossible to tell with what effect, as it was necessary to crawl through the plum bushes to get a view of our quarry.

After some consultation, ambitious Brown suggested that three of us go in, he taking the lead, Dozier and I following in single file. We had not proceeded far when the Indian shot, killing Brown. Dozier and I returned the fire, retreating at the same time to the clear. All was quiet then and we could not tell whether or not our shots had taken effect. One of our party then volunteered to make a circuit, and come around the back of the tree by crawling on his hands and knees. He had not been gone long when we heard another shot, and on looking over, found that he had been killed too. Some suggested that we simultaneously rush the Indian's hiding place, while others objected; and, as it was now getting dark, we decided to surround the spot, wait for morning and then fire the plum bushes and tall prairie grass, and burn him out. Morning came. One of the party crawling on his hands and knees to where Brown's body lay, found that he had been scalped. Then going to the other body, found that he, too, had been scalped and that the Indian had made his escape during the night. How that wily Indian could have so easily outwitted us, was a mystery to all. We secured the two bodies and returned to Deadwood, a tired and disgusted lot.

In the latter part of August a report was circulated that a great strike had been made at the base of what was called Sun Dance Mountain, situated about a hundred miles northwest of Deadwood. Myself and four others taking our saddle horses and a pack mule, started on the stampede. Those with me were Pat Kelly, Ed Milligan, Tom Dozier and Johnnie Varnes. We made Kelly captain. When going on dangerous trips we always selected some one of the party to act as captain, whose orders were obeyed to the letter. Kelly was a fighting Irishman and was not afraid of God, man or devil. The first night out an Indian could have killed us all with a butcher knife, as, having imbibed pretty freely during the day, we were in such condition that we slept like logs all night.

Three days after we left Deadwood, Milligan and myself were riding in advance about one-half mile. In looking down on the ground, I saw fresh pony tracks. We were about to ascend a hill at the time. I said, "Ed, those ponies have not passed here an hour. I can tell by the tracks, and if you will hold my horse, I will crawl up to the top of this ridge or hill and see what I can discover."

He did so. I looked over and there were about twenty-five Indians in the act of dismounting. They had with them some fifty head of good looking horses. I presumed they had stolen them. We started back and met the balance of the boys and reported to them what I had seen. Kelly, selecting a spot not far distant, where we went into camp; unpacked our mule, which had been packed with the outfit, and with our shovels dug a hole large enough to hold four of us, and a smaller one big enough for one man, he to hold the horses by their lariats, for we knew that we were to have a fight on our hands.

We did not get ready any too soon, for they came on the run, yelling as only Indians can yell. "Now," said Kelly, "don't fire a shot until I tell you."

We lay in our little fort with dirt thrown up as breastworks. The Indians rode to within a hundred or a hundred and fifty yards of us, then whirled and fired; Kelly still warning us not to shoot until ordered. A great trick of the Sioux is to get the whites to shoot their ammunition away and then he has them at his mercy. We had each forty rounds of ammunition and the only thing about our position was that we had no water. ' Otherwise, we had no fear of standing them off. After shooting at us they would again go back some distance and come again as before. They made a good many such charges. Finally two of their party, one a young fellow not more than twelve years old, I should judge, began to come a little nearer, shooting pretty close to us. The little fellow did not have a gun, but was using his bow and arrows. I said: "Kelly, I have always wanted to kill an Indian, and I wish you would let me have a shot at one of those fellows."

Kelly replied: "You take the big fellow and I will take the little one, if they come again."

I was delighted. They came again still closer than before. Kelly gave the word and we both fired, I hitting my man just under the ear and Kelly hitting his in the body. My man fell to the ground as dead as an oyster. Kelly's boy toppled over, but caught his pony's mane, holding himself on and disappeared behind a small hill, the others following. They seemed to have had enough of it.

We waited fully two hours and did not see any more of them. I then said to Kelly: "Kelly, I ran away from home when I was fourteen years of age with the intention of being a great Indian killer, and in all these years this is my first Indian, and I would like very much to take his scalp. Kelly agreed to my doing so.

We then all saddled up, riding up to the dead Indian, Kelly and I dismounting; I holding the scalp lock while Kelly cut it off. We did not make as fine a job of it as an Indian would have done, but I was satisfied. I had a scalp. Kelly took his war bonnet, Milligan his breech-clout, Varnes his moccasins and Dozier his gun. We then started for Deadwood. We had had enough of the stampeding business to last a while. We shared in the venture and trophies of war, but arrived in Deadwood with no gold.

I will now give you the balance of the history of that great female character, Calamity Jane.

Jane and I had not met since the return of the Jenny expedition to Fort Laramie, until one night when I was sitting in Jim Pencil's saloon playing faro bank someone tapped me on the shoulder. Looking around, I saw whom I supposed to be a young man dressed in buckskin, with a broad brimmed hat and two six-shooters. Turning again to the table I resumed my playing, when I was touched on the shoulder again. I then turned again and asked, "What do you want?"

The reply was, "Hello, Young, you know d— well you tried to drown me in Spring Creek."

It was Calamity Jane. She was alluding to the Jenny expedition episode, when I had upset the wagon with her in it. Her language was very profane and her love for whisky equalled that of any hard drinker. I asked her how she was fixed financially. She answered, "Dead broke." I gave her a five-dollar greenback, when she immediately proceeded to celebrate, and in a short time she was in a wild state of intoxication. She was then dubbed a good fellow and admitted as a member of the pioneer characters of Deadwood.

Her habits were thoroughly masculine. She danced with the dance-halls girls, as the balance of us did, associated with the men and showed no female traits whatever.

Swarringer, who kept the dance hall, was sorely in need of some new girls and employed Calamity to white slave for him. Fitting her out with a team, wagon and cooking utensils, he sent her to Nebraska to get a new supply of girls. At this business she was a huge success, the result of her first trip being ten girls. She had captivated them with exaggerated stories of the immense wealth in the Black Hills and the large amount of money to be made. She turned them over to Swarringer, retaining charge of them herself, educating and instructing them, and was in reality their friend as far as imposition was concerned. On one of her white slave trips she was stopped by the noted road agent, Jim Wall, and his confederates. She became enamored with one of the gang named Blackburn, who prevailed upon her to go with them. On her return to Deadwood she turned the team over to Swarringer and disappeared. A year later three of the gang were captured, and with them Calamity Jane. They were taken to Laramie City for trial, in the meantime being confined in a log jail, from which they made an attempt to escape by digging their way out under the jail, but were quickly recaptured while yet in the town. Her companions received long sentences, but for some unexplained reason, Calamity was not prosecuted. She lived for many years in various towns and mining camps in that country, following various occupations. She finally drifted back to Deadwood, entirely broken in body and spirits, and after a lingering illness of two years, during which all of her expenses were defrayed by the big-hearted town people, she passed away on August 2, 1906. On the same day and month, and the same hour, Wild Bill was

assassinated thirty years before. Her dying request
was that she be buried by the side of Wild Bill, which
was granted. And she now reposes by the side of him
whom she had for years greatly admired. May the
Supreme Ruler of the Universe forgive their faults,
for they had many virtues.

I will now give the reader a little inside history of
the massacre of that great man, General Custer, and
his regiment.

The news of this massacre was brought into Deadwood by courier, where I happened to be at the time.
From there it was telegraphed all over the world.
Much has been written regarding this massacre, but
it is all surmise, as no one escaped except one Crow
Indian scout, and his account of the massacre was so
muddled as to prove of no importance whatever; admitting himself that he was in the rocks when the
massacre occurred and that he did not see it at all.
The Sioux who did take part in it, on being questioned, gave very conflicting accounts of it, and being such infernal liars, drew on their imagination to
a large extent, so that no satisfaction was to be had
from them.

Personally, I was very sorry to learn of the trouble
between General Custer and the powers at Washington, for the General was a very fine soldier, both during the Civil and Indian wars, and I felt that in recog-
nition of his past services, his faults should have been
overlooked to a large extent; but such appears not
to have been the case.

In the late sixties there was a scandal in the frontier post known as the Belknap whisky case. Custer
was among the officers summoned to Washington to
give testimony regarding the scandal, and in a frank,
straightforward manner, told the truth. This met
with disfavor among certain high officials. Later on
Fred Grant graduated from West Point, and, owing

to the prominence of his father, was promoted from a second lieutenant to a lieutenant-colonel, being appointed on General Sheridan's staff. Custer expressed himself very freely on this rapid promotion, which placed him doubly wrong in the minds of the powers at Washington. Then it was decided that Custer must be humiliated.

The opportunity presented itself to carry out General Custer's humiliation during the Sioux war in 1876. General Miles was in command, and on two different occasions, Custer disobeyed orders. For these offenses he was to be court-martialed, and none knew this better than Custer himself; but he, being far in advance of the main command, it was difficult to get word to him to report at headquarters. Before he could be reached, his Crow Indian scouts reported a large band of Sioux on the Little Rose Bud River. Here Custer thought he saw his opportunity to win a big battle, one that would make him so popular and his standing such, as to recall the court martialling. He hurriedly consulted General Reno and formed a plan of attack. Reno with his command was to attack from the south, and Custer from the north, simultaneously. Shortly after separating, a large body of Sioux intercepted Reno, who, instead of showing fight, went into camp; but Custer, hearing the shooting, hurried on to fulfill his part, not knowing that Reno had gone into camp. After the Indians had stopped Reno, they immediately joined the main band. Custer made the charge, and not getting the assistance he expected from Reno, was annihilated with his brave followers, the seventh cavalry. Had Reno not shown the white feather but fought his way through, Custer and many of his command might have been alive today. Reno, having great influence at Washington, was not court-martialled for his cowardice, but was requested to resign, which he did.

CHAPTER XXIII.

THE FIRST SERMON IN DEADWOOD—FATE OF THE PREACHER—HE LOST BOTH HAIR AND GOLD DUST —WILD AND WOOLLY TIMES—THE INDIAN'S HEAD ON THE TOWN FLAGSTAFF—THE STORMS-VARNES DUEL—DEATH OF WILD BILL.

ONE Sunday there came walking into Deadwood an old man wearing a black slouched hat, a long, black coat, and holding in one hand a Bible. The old fellow was a preacher, of what denomination, I cannot state. No one there seemed to know where he came from. It being the Lord's Day, many miners had come into town to spend their gold dust. The preacher, thinking he might save a few souls, stopped in front of Jim Pencil's saloon, and standing on an empty box, began to preach. A large crowd gathered around the old fellow, listening to him very reverently. In the crowd were four or five dance-hall girls. This being the first preaching we had heard, it interested us very much. The old fellow held his hat in his left hand and his Bible in his right. He had not been preaching very long, when Calamity Jane, dressed in her buckskin attire and in an intoxicated condition, snatched his old hat from his hand, and turning to the crowd, addressed them thus:

"You sinners, dig down in your pokes, now; this old fellow looks as though he were broke and I want to collect about two hundred dollars for him. So limber up, boys."

She then started through the crowd and collected two hundred and thirty-five dollars in gold dust.

While collecting, the old man was still preaching. Calamity attempted to interrupt him by presenting him with his hat and gold dust. He motioned her aside. This offended her, and looking at him for a moment, she said:

"You d— old fool, take the money first and then proceed with your preaching."

I believe this shortened his sermon some, for he soon announced that he was going down to Crook City at the foothills, ten miles below Deadwood. Jack McAller, or Black Jack, told him that there were two routes to get there, one down the canyon and one by ascending the hill, then down the open plain; also told him that the Indians were bad and advised him to take the canyon route. The old man thanked him, and looking heavenward, said: "I trust in God, I know He will protect me."

Black Jack replied, "God is all right, but take my advice, parson," and offered a six-shooter to the old fellow, which the latter refused to touch. The parson then informed us he was going the hill route. Tying the gold dust in an old bandana handkerchief, he started up the hillside. When near the top, we saw him stop, and turning around facing us, he extended both hands in the air as though he were blessing us, then disappeared over the hill.

In about three hours two men arrived in town very much excited, stating that they had found the body of an old man killed and scalped, with a gun shot in his back and an arrow piercing his neck. We knew at once it was the parson. Going out there, we found the body minus the gold dust. We brought him in, and buried him on a flat in the rear of the Montana saloon. Later we learned that he was the Reverend Hiram Weston Smith. He was the first man to plant the seed of Christianity in the Black Hills. I understand that there are now five churches in Deadwood. The citizens of Deadwood eight years later moved the

body to a new cemetery and erected a monument to
his memory, with the inscription: "Here lines the
Reverend Hiram Weston Smith, killed by Indians,
August 22, 1876,—the Pioneer Preacher of the Black
Hills."

The Sioux Indians were very troublesome to the
residents of Deadwood. Coming from the plains, they
would secret themselves behind rocks on the ridge top
and shoot into town. The citizens finally offered a
reward of five hundred dollars for the first Indian
scalp brought into Deadwood. Two Mexicans, wending their way by the hill route to Deadwood, having
started from Crook City, killed an Indian, who was
about twenty-five years of age, I should judge. Instead of scalping him, they cut his head off, carrying
it by the scalp lock and walked into town. A great
crowd followed them into the saloon where I worked.

I had my back to the entrance of the saloon, and
upon hearing the commotion I suddenly turned around,
and on the bar sat the Indian head, the Mexican holding it there with his hands. The face was painted,
the upper side with little black dots, and the
lower portion red. In his ears he wore ear rings, and
he had been quite hansome for an Indian. The Mexican asked me where he was to receive the reward.
Just then Black Jack stepped up, telling him that he
would pay the money, which he did, suggesting that
we have a celebration, and to which the crowd agreed.

We then started on a visit to all the saloons. Jack
and Calamity Jane led the way, Jack carrying the
head and Calamity doing the yelling, haranguing the
crowd. Our tour included all the dance halls and
business houses, and we kept this performance up all
night. All having imbibed freely, when morning came
Calamity suggested that we hoist the head up on the
flagstaff, which had previously been erected. We

started our procession to the upper end of town, and there never had been and never will be such a scene enacted on earth again. When we arrived at the designated spot, they attached the flag halyard to the scalp lock and with a whoop, Calamity and Jack hoisted it up. We then formed a great circle around the flagstaff and no body of Sioux Indians ever equaled that war dance. This lasted for a solid hour, when they lowered it down and buried it. This ended the grand celebration of the Indian's head.

The following morning a man notified us that he had found the bodies of the two Mexicans who had killed and brought this Indian head into town. They were lying close together, each with a six-shooter in his right hand, with an empty chamber in each gun. We concluded that they had quarreled over the distribution of the five hundred dollars and had shot at one another about the same time, killing each other. We buried them alongside the Indian head. This was a remarkable coincident.

Two gamblers named Charley Storms and Johnnie Varnes, while playing cards, had a misunderstanding. Both being brave men, they agreed to go out on the street and fight a duel with six-shooters. Varnes carried the first double-acting gun I ever saw, called a Whistler. It was of English make. It was quite short and shot a very large calibre ball. Storms carried a Colts forty-five.

Standing in line, Varnes' position being near the running gear of a wagon, rested this gun on the top of the wagon wheel, shooting at Storms very rapidly, Storms shooting but two shots at Varnes, both striking the wagon tire below Varnes' head, bounding over it. This saved Varnes. One of Varnes' shots struck a German in the hip. The German was standing about twenty steps out of line, but Varnes' gun being so short and of such heavy calibre, shot anywhere rather than where he pointed it. When Varnes' gun was emptied he threw up his hands, telling Storms so.

The latter replied, "Go get a better gun. You cannot hit a barn door with that one."

In the meantime friends interferred, stopping the duel, and they afterward became great friends. Poor Storms was killed years later in Tombstone, Arizona, by Luke Short, a faro dealer. Varnes died in Denver, Colorado, an opium fiend, and thus ended two brave men.

About the middle of June there arrived in Deadwood my old friend, "Wild Bill." Accompanying him was Charley Utter, commonly known as Colorado Charley. They were mounted and a more picturesque sight could not be imagined than Wild Bill on horseback. This character had never been north of Cheyenne before this, for he originated in the south, as previously stated. Many in Deadwood knew him, having met him before; others knew him only by reputationfi particularly those who came from Montana.

Among these Montana people were a good many men of note. I mean by that, gun men, and the arrival of this character in town caused quite a commotion. They rode up to the saloon where I was working, both of them having known Carl Mann before; he being a great friend of Bills', they naturally called on him first. They dismounted and walked into the saloon, great crowds following them until the room was packed. Mann cordially received them, asking them to make this saloon their headquarters, which they agreed to do. This meant money to Mann, as Bill would be a great drawing card.

After the excitement of Bill's arrival had subsided a little, Bill looked at me a few moments, then said: "Kid, here• you are again, like the bad penny, but I am awfully glad to see you." And turning to Carl Mann, remarked: "I first met this kid in Hayes City, Kansas, and wherever I go, he seems to precede me or to follow me, for I have met him in Abeline, Ellsworth, Cheyenne, and now again here; but he is a good boy and you can trust him. Take my word for that."

Bill's occupation at this time was that of a gambler. Since I had last seen him, he seemed to have changed greatly and tried very hard to avoid notoriety, conducting himself in a very gentlemanly manner, but unfortunately his past reputation was still a matter of public comment. Consequently, he was subjected to a great deal of criticism, pro and con. At this time there were many gun fighters in Deadwood, the majority of which hailed from Montana. Knowing Bill only by reputation, they misjudged him to a marked degree. To have the reader more clearly understand their relative positions to each other, I will say that Bill had attained much the same reputation as a prize fighter who had successfully sent all of his opponents down to defeat and become the acknowledged champion. Professional gun fighters in those days aspired to kill any one of their number who had the record of being their superior, and by thus doing, claimed the so-called championship.

One night in June a party of six Montana men congregated in the Montana saloon and engaged in a general spirited talk of criticism, the target of their remarks being Bill. A friend of his happened to be in the saloon and lost no time in going to the Sixty-six saloon where he found Bill, and told him what he had heard. In supreme disgust, Bill went immediately to the Montana saloon and walking up to the crowd, remarked:

"I understand that you cheap, would-be gun fighters from Montana have been making remarks about me, and I want you all to understand that unless they are stopped there will shortly be a number of cheap funerals in Deadwood. I have come to this town not to court notoriety or villianous talk, but to live in peace, and do not propose to stand for your insults."

Having thus declared himself, Bill ordered the entire six to line up against the wall and deliver up their guns, which they quickly did in a very sheepish manner. Bill had accomplished his purpose without the flash of a gun on his part. Backing out of the saloon, he leisurely walked down the street to the Sixty-six saloon and resumed his seat at the card table. This act, of course, became the talk of the town.

Seeing much of Bill every day and being a very close observer, I became familiar with many of his characteristics, some of which are worthy of special mention.

In drinking at a bar, Bill invariably poured out the whisky with his left hand, his right being free for possible emergency. He was careful to face all with whom he was drinking, and under no circumstances would he chance any one being behind him. In a card game he always sat with his back to the wall. I have often thought of the constant uneasiness that he must have felt at all times.

There was also the comic side to Bill's nature, which asserted itself in his jovial moods, and his stories at such times made up by himself, for he was a great story teller, were highly entertaining. I will narrate two of them as related to us. On this occasion Bill had been asked for a story by a crowd who knew him by reputation only and appreciated the fact that his stories would be a rare treat. Bill responded as follows:

"Some years ago in the Indian territory I was scouting for General Custer, and getting up into southwestern Kansas, which was a new country to me at that time, I was riding quite a distance ahead of the command, when I saw an opening about two feet wide which seemed to run into a bluff. I thought I would explore this. On closer examination I found this passageway about ten feet long. Passing through it I discovered that it led to a large, open space of considerable area and was surrounded on all sides by a wall. I remarked to myself, what a great protection from Indians this would be if one were hard pressed,—the entrance being so narrow, one could secrete himself on the inside and kill any number of them, as they could only enter one at a time. I was armed with a six-shooter and also a large knife. The thought had hardly passed through my brain, when in looking at the entrance I saw an Indian approaching. Knowing he was hostile, I shot him. Another came; I also shot him. They kept coming one by one until I had discharged the six shots that my gun contained. In those days we used the powder and ball six-shooters, with caps on the nipples. Not having any extra ammunition with me, I was unable to reload. More Indians kept coming. I then drew my knife from my belt and backed up against the wall at the farther end, while in the meantime the open space became crowded with Indians."

Here, Bill stopped telling the story. One of the many listeners, however, asked him what he did then. Bill hesitated a moment, then replied:

"What could I do? There were many of them, well armed, and I had only my knife."

"Well, then," questioned his interrogator, "what did they do?"

Bill gave a long sigh, saying: "By God, they killed me, boys!"

For a few moments they did not seem to see the joke, but soon began laughing. One of them asked the crowd up to the bar to drink, Bill whispering to me:

"Kid, that's one time I had to die."

I replied, "Why didn't you unfold your wings and fly?"

He said the next time he told that story he would escape in that manner.

At another time Bill told the following story: He was riding along one day in the mountains in Colorado and was about to cross an open space, when he heard a loud noise behind him. Looking back, he saw a great snake about fifty feet long, with a head resembling a man's—having the nose, mouth and chin of a man, also a pair of legs, which looked very much like a man's arms; its breast and stomach both resembled those of a man also. It was a vicious looking reptile. His horse scenting it, became frightened and ran away with him. The faster the horse ran, the closer this reptile approached, convincing Bill that it would soon catch up with him. Turning in his saddle, he shot the reptile dead. Quieting his horse, he dismounted and with his gun in hand ready for immediate use, he walked back to examine the reptile, and found that it really had a stomach like a human being. He could not carry it with him to camp, so cut the head off; then opening the stomach, found in there eight hundred and seventy-five dollars worth of gold dust. This was a gold eating snake. Now he was in a quandry, not daring to take the head back with him as he might be compelled to give up the gold, so he decided to cover it up with earth at a nearby bluff. Going to the nearest town, he displayed this gold dust, not telling where he had procured it, but the people then began prospecting for gold in Colorado and discovered it in paying quantities. And this gold eating snake should have the credit for the discovery. "This is the first time I have ever told the secret," added Bill.

I thought the listeners would explode with laughter, which pleased Bill very much.

Early one morning two days before Bill's assassination, he walked into the Sixty-six saloon. We were alone at the time and I noticed he looked very dejected. I remarked, "Bill, you are not looking very well this morning."

"No," he replied. "I have a feeling that something is going to happen to me."

I remarked, "Bill, you are drinking too much."

"No," he answered, "that has nothing to do with it. I have had this feeling for two weeks, but know I will never be killed by any one in front of me and if it does come, it will be from the back. Now, I want you to do something for me. Step out here and walk backward until I tell you to stop." I did so until he told me to halt. This being a very peculiar request on his part, I asked him the reason for it. He told me that his eye sight was failing him, and he wanted to satisfy himself as to the distance that he could distinguish a man. He then said: "Two steps before you stopped, I could plainly recognize you, after which I could see nothing but a' blur. Don't mention this circumstance to any one as I do not care to have it known."

To give the reader some idea of the rapidity and accuracy with which Bill could shoot—first bear in mind that six shooters in his time were not cartridge guns nor were they double action. One had to load them with powder and ball and place caps on the nipples attached to the cylinders, and had to cock the hammer each time he shot.

In 1868 he was riding from Hays City to Fort Hays, in company with General Custer. In passing a telegraph pole Bill remarked to Custer, "General, would you believe that I could ride past one of these poles on the run and shoot six shots into it with my six shooter and that you could cover the space where I hit it with the palm of your hand?"

"No," Custer replied, "no man could accomplish such a feat." Bill put spurs to his horse, and when opposite a pole, shot six shots into it, and sure enough on examination, Custer found he had hit it six times, and that he could cover the spot with his hand. When they arrived at the Fort, Custer had a tin sign made, verifying the fact, and had the sign nailed to the pole. If the reader should at any time visit Hays, Kansas, he will find the pole still there, the citizens of Hays having had it cemented in the ground. They keep it in preservation as an old time relic of this wonderful character.

On the night of August 1st, 1876, he was playing cards with a miner named Jack McCall, who was a worthless character and decidedly repulsive, being cross-eyed to such an extent that it was hard to tell which way he was looking. On the morning of the 2nd, I came on watch, relieving the night man, and found them still playing cards. The night man told me they had been playing since midnight and that McCall was about broke, at the same time showing me McCall's sack of gold dust that lay behind the bar. Presently Bill asked me how much dust was in the sack. I weighed it and told him one hundred and seven dollars worth.

Bill then remarked to McCall: "You have overplayed yourself by ten dollars."

McCall replied, "All right, I will make it good next Saturday night."

This ended the game, McCall saying "I have not got money enough to buy my breakfast." Bill handed him seventy-five cents in shinplasters, telling him to go and eat; also telling him that if he got hungry again later in the day, he would help him out. They then had a parting drink together, and McCall left the saloon.

About one-thirty in the afternoon, Carl Mann, Charley Rich and Captain Massey engaged in a poker game. Bill, in company with Charley Utter sauntered in and was invited by Mann to make the game four-handed. Bill joined them, but before doing so requested Rich, who was sitting with his back to the wall, to give him his seat. Knowing Bill's habits, Rich rose to comply, when Captain Massey, from whom Bill had won some money a few nights before, spoke up and said that he preferred to have Bill sit opposite him, remarking: "No one is going to shoot you in the back."

Bill replied, "All right, you old grouch. I will sit here," at the same time pulling out the stool with his foot, from under the table, sitting down on it. Mann sat on Bill's left, Rich on his right and Massey opposite, Bill facing the front entrance to the saloon, with his back exposed to the rear entrance. They had been playing not to exceed twenty minutes, when Massey beat a king full for Bill with four sevens, breaking Bill on the hand. They were playing table stakes. Bill then asked me to bring him fifty dollars worth of checks, which I did. Charley Utter, who had been sitting by Bill's side a little back of him, remarked: "Bill, I will go and get something to eat." I placed the checks on the table in front of Bill, standing as I did so between him and Carl Mann. Bill looked up at me and remarked: "The old duffer (meaning Massey) broke me on the hand." These were the last words he ever uttered.

There was a loud report, followed by the words, "Take that." McCall had shot him in the back of the head with a forty-five Colts six-shooter, the ball coming out under the right cheek bone, and piercing the wrist of Captain Massey, who had his hand around his checks that he had just won from Bill.

Massey was the first to run out to the street, shouting that Wild Bill had shot him. He did not know differently until some time afterward. No one being armed at the time, we all rushed out to the street, McCall following. The latter tried to make his escape on a horse, which was tied to a hitching rack in front of the door. The cinch of the saddle having been loosened, when he attempted to mount the horse, the saddle turned with him. He then ran out into the middle of the street. By this time a large crowd had gathered, which surrounded him. With six-shooter in his hand, McCall pointed first at one and then another, but not shooting. Those in the crowd who were armed were afraid to shoot at him for fear of shooting each other. A man named Tom Mulquinn grasped him from behind, pinned his arms while the others disarmed him. They then took him back into the saloon where the body lay and asked him a few questions, which he refused to answer. They finally took him to a log cabin in the rear of the saloon. All was excitement. Some wanted to hang him, others to shoot him, but wiser heads prevailed and an investigation was agreed upon. He was kept under guard for three days and then given a miner's trial in the opera house. Selecting twelve men as a jury, a man to prosecute and another to defend him, for by this time, on account of Bill's past reputation, the citizens split into two factions, one of which sympathized with McCall and the other faction with Bill.

After the witnesses had been examined, McCall took the stand in his own defense and told in a straightforward manner that Bill had killed his brother, Sam Strawhan, in Riley's saloon at Hayes City, Kansas, in 1868, while he was a soldier at Fort Hayes; that he had promised his widowed mother on her death bed he would follow Bill as long as he lived till he got a chance to kill him, and knowing Bill's reputation for quickness with a gun, knew that his only chance was to slip up behind him. He admitted that he had killed Bill, was glad of it, and would do the same thing over again if he had to. The jury believed the statement and acquitted him.

McCall left Deadwood that same night, going to Laramie City on the Union Pacific railroad, and there boasted of the killing of Wild Bill. A friend of Bill's telegraphed to Jeff Carr at Cheyenne, then United States Marshal of Wyoming, who arrested McCall. He was taken to Yankton, South Dakota, tried before the United States Court, convicted and hanged.

On the scaffold McCall denied the previous statement that Strawhan was his brother and admitted that he had told the story to fool the Deadwood miners. He said that he was a deserter from the 7th cavalry, but that he was in Hayes City at the time Bill killed Strawhan, and that he did not know why he killed Bill, as he had never done him any harm. His hanging was spectacular. A scaffold was erected on the open prairie and thousands of people from miles around witnessed the execution.

Wild Bill's body was buried with his head resting near a large pine stump, on which was blazed the following inscription: "Here lies the body of Wild Bill, murdered by Jack McCall, August the 2nd, 1876." Underneath this the words: "Custer was lonesome without you."

The funeral was a very large one, and very impressive; all the stores, saloons and dance-halls being closed out of respect to the greatest character of his day.

Eight years later the citizens of Deadwood moved all the bodies of the dead to a new cemetery. On exhuming Bill's body, his entire left side was found to be petrified. Bill's body and that of Parson Smith were buried side by side, and monuments erected over them as a mark of honor and respect. And to this day, I am told, on the second day of August, the bells are tolled in Deadwood. Two monuments were made for Bill. The first one was completely destroyed by being chipped by tourists and curio hunters. The present monument is protected by a steel wire enclosure.

Wild Bill didn't in his career as a marshal impose on men because he was such. I will sight an instance. While at Hayes City, one Hughie Teets kept a butcher shop in that town, and had some hot words with Bill, finally saying, "Bill, if you will put your guns away I will fight you a fist fight."

"All right," replied Bill, handing his guns to a friend. They went at it hammer and tongs. First Bill would have the best of it, and again Hughie. Finally Hughie backed Bill up against the sidewalk, which was about four feet higher than the street. Bending Bill back against the walk, he was pounding him unmercifully, when outsiders interfered. Hughie would not quit unless Bill would cry enough. This Bill refused to do. Finally the crowd, fearing that Hughie would break Bill's back, pulled him off Bill, who arose quietly putting his hands against his back, saying, "Hughie, you came d—— near breaking my back, but I still think I am the better man, and when I fully recover from this scrap, I will fight you again, but it will be on the prairie where there are no sidewalks."

Hughie replied, "All right, Bill, I will be ready any-time you feel like it." Some weeks after Bill called on Hughie, and said, "I have thought this matter over and have concluded to call it off, as I believe you are as good a man as I." This ended the matter. Hughie now resides in Portland, Oregon, hale and hearty at 76 years of age.

CHAPTER XXIV.

PERILS OF THE TRAIL—A RIDE WITH DISPATCHES—
THE HORSE A FAITHFUL SENTINEL—COMIC HAP-
PENINGS IN DEADWOOD.

ABOUT the middle of August there arrived in Deadwood a courier with dispatches from General Miles' command. This fellow had ridden some four hundred miles and was very sick with mountain fever. Being unable to continue his journey to Fort Laramie, and it being necessary to get those dispatches to their destination, he tried to secure someone to carry them through. Hearing of this, I received permission from Mr. Mann to make the trip to Fort Laramie, where I had some business I wanted to attend to.

The courier gave me the dispatches and an order on the commanding officer for one hundred dollars; this amount was to be deducted from the money he was to receive. In making these rides one is compelled to ride nights, laying up in the day time, owing to the Indians being bad. I left Deadwood at nine o'clock P. M., and rode until just before day break. After watering my horse, I staked him out by driving a large picket pin in the ground, attaching to it a forty foot lariat tied to the horse's neck. This gave him space enough to graze. I then took my saddle, bridle and saddle blanket, going off some five hundred yards from the horse, where I lay down to sleep—or, to try to sleep. With the thought of danger in mind, I did not expect to sleep soundly. The reason for my getting some distance away from the horse I will explain:

If an Indian or Indians discovered a horse, they would straightway look for the owner and by being hidden in this manner, one would be less liable to discovery and had a better chance of defending himself, as a Sioux Indian did not care to take an even chance, and would be more likely to take the horse than to hunt for its rider. Before approaching the horse in the evening about dusk, the rider arose carefully, looking at the horse and if he were lying down or grazing, the rider could be pretty certain that there were no Indians in very close proximity to him. On the other hand, if he were looking in any particular direction, and scented danger, he would throw his ears forward and if convinced that the object he was looking at was an Indian, he would run at top speed around the picket pin, trying to escape. It would be then that the rider must look out for himself. If any of these things did not happen, he would walk over to the horse, saddle him, water him, and resume his journey.

It is wonderful when one is out with these animals, how attached they become. There were times when I would walk up to my horse, that he would nicker in a low tone and rub his nose against me in a very knowing manner. Meaning, I presume, "I am glad to see you." The third night out on this trip, the night being very dark, I was riding through Red Canyon at a rapid pace. This was a very dangerous part of the road, as the canyon was deep and one each side very rocky hills; along the water's edge large willows grew, the road crossing a stream at four different points.

Suddenly my horse shied, snorted and stopped, and came very near unseating me. I tried to urge him on but he would not move. Dismounting, and holding him by the bridle rein, I walked a step or two and found lying in their blankets, on the ground, a man and woman, killed and scalped. The Indians must have crawled upon them while they were asleep, as I saw no signs of a struggle. Hurriedly mounting my horse, I went on until I reached the end of the canyon, where there was a company of soldiers stationed to escort teams through this canyon and protect them. I told them of what I had seen and remained there during the day. About ten o'clock in the morning they brought the bodies there and found in addition to what I saw, another body—that of a negro woman. She too had been killed and scalped. I arrived in Fort Laramie in due time, delivering my dispatches and collecting my money. I remained there three days, returning to Deadwood with some freighters who were hauling freight. We had a very pleasant trip.

Combined with a rough occurrences in Deadwood, we also had many innocent amusements, some of which were very comical. I have spoken of a character named Cheating Sheely, so named on account of his being a great cheat at cards. It was utterly impossible for him to play cards for money or fun without cheating. He was our porter in the saloon, and received his pay every night—five dollars. He would then leave the saloon looking for some easy victim with whom to play cards. Cheeting Sheely invariably lost, as he was so busy cheating that he neglected to watch the actions of his opponents, who could also cheat, in many cases. However, one night he found an easy game in which he won three hundred dollars in gold dust. He now thought he had all the money in Deadwood. In order to win this he was compelled to play all night. When showing up at the saloon in the morning, he was so sleepy that he could scarcely keep his eyes open. The news of his winning was well known around the saloon. About three o'clock in the afternoon, he lay down on a bench at the rear of the room, taking off his coat and vest, which contained his money, and folding them up, placed them under his head for a pillow. Carl Mann, who was a great practical joker, seeing him sleeping there, concluded to give him a scare, and if possible get possession of his gold. Gathering all the stools that we had in the house (we did not have chairs in those days), he piled them up over Sheely in such a manner that if he moved they would fall. Mann then took his six-shooter and fired it through the open back door.

Sheely being an awful coward and having a great fear of a six-shooter, when the report aroused him, suddenly jumped up, knocking over the stools, rushing out of the back door, calling out that he had been shot. Carl Mann then hurriedly took his poke of dust from his coat, substituting one of the same size, containing brass filings and other material. In a short time Sheely returned and picking up his coat, extracted the poke, saying it was a wonder some one had not stolen it. He then went off to bed without examining the contents. He returned in about an hour, his face as white as marble, exhibited the poke, and showed us its contents. We all laughed. Carl Mann told him to go after the fellow he had played cards with, as he was sure it was he who had buncoed him. For two days he hunted for this man. Carl Mann, being afraid Sheely would go crazy, returned his money.

Another character, Pink Bedford, was a very fine poker player, and if sober, was capable of winning large sums of money. But poor Pink would go on periodical sprees, lasting until he would finally become sick. Carl Mann was much interested in this man and tried in many ways to keep him straight, but always failing. Finally he concluded that he would have a joke on him.

Procuring a ladder about twenty-five feet long, Carl Mann and two others lashed Pink on it, with his feet resting on a round of the ladder, his arms being lashed to the side, allowing him space enough to bend his head over. They then took the ladder out in the street, setting it up against the building. When Pink sobered up a little, he could not understand where he was and began to yell. Mann ran out and threw a bucket of water in his face. This revived him very much. Mann then addressed him thus: "You must promise me that you will not drink whiskey again for six months and you must swear that you will not." Pink took some horrible oaths, one of them being that he hoped God would paralyze him if he took another drink of whiskey for six months.

They then carried him to the rear of the dance-hall, standing the ladder against the door which opened in. The dance-hall girls lived in this end of the building. The manager, or bouncer as he was termed, stepping outside, hollered to the girls to come out there quick. When they opened the door, the ladder and Pink, naturally fell in on them. This frightened them very much. Pink begged for dear life to be released, but before doing so, they carried him through the dance-hall, finally bringing him over to the saloon and releasing him.

Pink then behaved himself for about two weeks. One day, however, on going into the Montana saloon, one of his friends saw him setting a glass down on the bar, having just taken a drink. This friend then said to him: "Take a drink with me."

Looking at his friend a moment, he said: "Do not tempt me. Don't you know I have sworn off drinking whiskey."

His friend then said: "Take a cigar or something soft?"

Pink, turning to the barkeeper, asked him to give him a drink of gin. Carl Mann, hearing of this, immediately went after him, reminding him of the oaths he had taken. After looking at Mann a few moments, he said: "It was gin I drank, and I have no recollection of taking an oath only that I would not take a drink of whiskey for six months, which I intend to keep." This amused Mann very much. Poor Pink could not keep away from the booze, which was his undoing.

In front of the window, outside of the Sixty-six saloon, Mann had a bench erected, which would accommodate two people only. In one end of this he bored a small hole through it, placing therein a needle pointing up, attaching to the head of the needle a small weight, and then running the string through the window to the inside of the building. Then he would get someone in conversation, sitting him down on the end where the needle was. Mann would have some confederate pull the string, which would pierce the one sitting there, the weight pulling the needle down. The hole in the bench was so small that it was not perceptible, the victim getting pierced, would jump up and with his hand feel on the bench and then to the part of his anatomy pierced, and many times would finally conclude that it was a sliver or something else, and would again sit down, when he would be pierced a second time. This caused a great deal of laughter, forcing the victim to buy the drinks for those present. The boys around the saloon worked this very strong, particularly one named Johnie the Oyster, so Carl Mann one day reversed the needle in the bench. Oyster coming along with a victim and not knowing that the needle had been changed, set his man down and began talking to him, when Carl pulled the string, piercing Oyster very hard. Oyster jumped in the air about three feet, yelling with pain. The fellow with him thought that he had gone crazy, and I don't wonder, for Oyster was tearing around there, threatening to kill everybody in the saloon. However, in time he quieted down, treated everybody, and the bench was removed.

I left Deadwood October 1st, 1876, in company with twenty others. We were employed by my friend Botsford and the Wheeler Bros. to guard two thousand pounds of gold dust they were taking from Deadwood to Cheyenne, as rumors had been circulated that road agents planned to hold up the same. The gold dust was transported in a four-horse wagon. We guards were mounted and heavily armed; five others and myself riding a quarter of a mile ahead as advance guards and five others acting as rear guards, the balance riding each side of the wagon.

We made this trip in very fast time, arriving in Cheyenne without any incident out of the ordinary. The owners of the gold dust paid us each two hundred dollars and a railroad ticket to any point desired. The owners went to the Centennial at Philadelphia, transporting their gold dust with them. I took my ticket to Eureka, Nevada, arriving there in due course of time with over five thousand dollars in my possession. There I met an old miner, who had partially developed a silver mine at a place called Tybo, two hundred miles south of Eureka. He gave me a half interest and together we went to develop it, I furnishing the capital. In three months I was broke, the mine proving a failure. I worked my way back to Eureka and from there to Winnemucca, Nevada, where I found a stock man who was transporting ten carloads of cattle to Oakland, California. He employed me to help care for them en route, giving me my passage and board. He kept telling me how valuable I was to him and that when he unloaded at Oakland, he would not forget me financially, as he knew I was broke.

After unloading the cattle, he gave me his residence address in Oakland, telling me to be there at

five o'clock and if he was not there, that he would
leave the money for me with his wife. I was at his
house at the appointed time and was met at the door
by his wife, who said: "Oh, you are the man who
came with my husband on the cattle train. He is not
in, but has left something for you." Whereupon she
generously handed me the munificent sum of thirty-
five cents.

I took the money, looked at the woman in astonishment and said: "Is this all he left?"

"Why, yes," she replied. "What did you expect;
a million dollars?"

"No, no," I answered, "this will last me the balance
of my life." I shall always believe that she held out
a portion of the money, or else her husband had
peddled me a large amount of hot air during the trip.

I crossed the ferry to San Francisco at a cost
of fifteen cents, and was at last in a city of the
Golden West, with a handbag and a capital of twenty
cents with which to start life anew. This was in
1877. Passing through the ferry station, it being
about nine o'clock in the evening, I was accosted by
one of the night-hawk hackmen, so numerous in those
days. He snatched my bag from my hand, opened the
hack door and insisted on my getting in. I immediately recognized him as a man called Slippery Smith,
who the year before had been run out of Deadwood for
horse stealing and who was an all-round tough character. He had not recognized me.

Chuckling to myself, I got into his hack. He did
not ask me where I wanted to go, but drove me
around for half an hour, finally stopping in front of
the Grand Hotel. Before opening the hack door, he
demanded my fare, which he said was five dollars. I
then asked him to drive me to the city jail.

This was a puzzler to Slippery Smith, and he asked me why I wanted to go there.

I replied: "To have you arrested for stealing horses in Deadwood."

He then opened the hack door and under the street light looked me carefully over, and finally recognized me. Grasping me by the hand, shaking it 'till it was nearly torn from the sockets, he remarked: "Young, I am glad to see you. What in the world are you doing here?" I then told him my late experiences, also that my finances were reduced to twenty cents. He insisted upon my getting back into the hack, and drove to a restaurant where we partook of a fine meal. We then went to his room; Smith telling me to go to bed and that he would see me in the morning. This I did, and got a good night's rest.

The reader must bear in mind that this was my first appearance in a large, civilized city for a number of years. My friend arrived at the room about nine o'clock in the morning and took me to breakfast, where we talked over old times in Deadwood. Handing me a five dollar gold piece and giving me the address of the house, he told me to take in the sights and enjoy myself, and meet him at the room at six o'clock. I wandered around all day like a stray goose and wondering why in the vast crowd of people I met and passed there was not a single familiar face.

Completely tired out, six o'clock finally came. I found the room and my friend Smith waiting for me. On the way to supper he informed me that he would take care of me until I was accustomed to city ways, and that the better way for me to do would be to accompany him on his hack. I accepted his suggestion, and became what he termed the "hack dog." I did not ask him at the time the meaning of the term, but very soon found out by a little experience on the third night. Our hack stand was at the corner of Bush and Kearney Streets and the business usually commenced at about two o'clock in the morning, after the horse-cars had stopped running. We were then on the alert for unfortunates, who, having imbibed too freely, had missed the last car.

This particular morning we grabbed an athletic appearing young man, whom we put in the hack, and after considerable questioning got from him his address. After driving him around for about an hour, we eventually took him to his destination. The long ride had partially sobered him. On getting out of the hack, Smith demanded seven dollars, at the same time trying to impress upon the young man the fact that he had been driven to various places and that the charge was reasonable. I was sitting on the hack seat at the time and saw him knock Smith under the hack. This was where the part of the "hack dog" came in, as I was supposed to go to the assistance of the driver. This I quickly did, and had no sooner landed on the sidewalk, when the athlete landed on me, with a knockout blow between the eyes, putting me to sleep.

When I came to, I found Smith still much dazed and our passenger gone. Both of my eyes were badly swollen and for the next few days very black. The next day in the room, Smith remarked: "That fellow was a corker." And I heartily agreed with him.

I followed the hack-dog business for about a month, and I assure you had many funny experiences. At times when the passengers would not settle the exhorbitant fares, Smith would drive them to the nearest policeman and if they had money on them, he would force them to settle; the policeman receiving a portion of the fare collected. If they did not have the money, we would take their watch, ring or any article of value, telling them that they could redeem such article at the hack stand at the corner of Bush and Kearney Streets. This they invariably did. While I appreciated Smith's kindness, the business was not to my liking, and I could not get used to city life. Consequently when harvest time came, I severed my connections with him and left the busy city for life I was more adapted to.

While out in the harvest field, I became acquainted with a man from Portland, Oregon, who told me of the many chances for a young man in that city. After harvest, I returned to San Francisco and from there took the steamer to Portland. In 1879, one year after my arrival in Portland, I was fortunate enough to get a position which in many respects was similar to my past experience and much like the work I had been accustomed to.

The construction of the Northern Pacific railroad was in progress, through the sparcely settled country of Eastern Oregon, Idaho and Montana. My position was that of riding steward for the firm of Du Boise & King, who had the contract for the boarding of the white men on the construction. Having had experience on the construction of the Atchison, Topeka & Santa Fe railroad, I thoroughly understood the type of men I would have to deal with. They were principally Irish and I found among them many of whom had worked on the Santa Fe in the same line of work. To the Irish we must give the credit of building the first transcontinental railroad. I often wonder what has become of this vast army of men, for they seem to have entirely disappeared, as far as construction work is concerned. It must be that they have been supplanted by the Italians and Japs.

We boarded these men in large tents. At times there were as many as two hundred in one camp and about thirty camps strung along the construction work for a distance of twenty-five miles or more. It was my duty to keep these camps supplied with food, cooks and waiters. We used tin dishes. As the construction work advanced, tents had to be moved. Our supplies were shipped from Portland to the end of the track and from there transported by four-horse teams. These men were a hard set of people to handle and made more so as whiskey was allowed to be sold in each camp.

The reader can imagine approximately six thousand of these men being paid off on the first of each month, less four dollars and fifty cents per week each reserved for board. After being paid, the majority of them would go to the saloon, get beastly intoxicated and then settle any previous differences which might have arisen, by fighting like bulldogs. This was the particular time when they were looking for the riding stewart, blaming him for the poor quality of food and numerous other things, and winding up with threats of dire vengeance. There was no turning back on the part of the steward, for he had to meet them every day whether they were drunk or sober. And I assure you it required a good deal of tact and nerve for him to do so. I was mounted but not armed and had to be guided entirely by diplomacy. I will cite one of many instances during the year I filled this position.

One morning at about four o'clock—five days after payday—I was within about a mile of Camp No. 25 (each camp being numbered), when I heard a man groaning in the brush by the roadside. Dismounting, I found an old man named Pat Malloy, who ran one of the saloons at this camp. He had been badly beaten up by these fellows, and informed me that they had raided his saloon, demolishing everything and confiscated his whiskey. He begged of me not to go into this camp, as they were planning on hanging the riding steward when he came along. I thanked the old fellow for the warning, but told him that I must visit the camp, which I did. I found a great crowd congregated there, formed in a circle, and in the center two men stripped to the waist were engaged in the so-called manly art of prize fighting. They had whiskey in tin buckets from which they were drinking freely.

I rode up to the rear of the tent (they being out in front) and after tying my horse to a post, I entered. And such a sight I beheld! Tables turned over, dishes and cooking utensils scattered about, and the cooks and waiters gone. Not having had breakfast, I found a couple of biscuits and began to eat. Up to this time I had not been noticed. Presently someone called out, "Boys, here is the riding steward's horse. Let's find the steward and hang him." Then led by a big, strapping Irishman, they rushed into the tent. I stood my ground and putting up my hand and in a loud voice commaned them to stop, as I had something to say. Their leader checked them, saying, "Let him talk. For it is the last talk he will make on earth."

I began, "Boys, I am just the same as one of you, and working for wages the same as you are." (What followed verifies the biblical quotation, "Cast your bread upon the waters and it shall return tenfold.")

Before I ceased talking, the leader suddenly raised his hand, saying: "Boys, yez shall not touch that boy. for, in the old Nicolai House in Portland, he gave me a bed and twenty-five cents to get my breakfast in the morning. If yez touch him, yez will have to fight me." This stopped them. They took me by the arm, in a friendly spirit, rushed me to the liquor refreshments, insisting that I have a drink, then another, which I accepted. They then appointed me referee of two fights that followed. After imbibing this bad, fighting whiskey, I was sorely tempted to go a round myself, but instead I hunted up the camp crew, finding them a mile down the road, hiding in the brush and badly frightened. After a good deal of persuasion on my part, I succeeded in getting them back to the camp. Straightening up the wreckage and getting the fire started, I waited for them to cook a meal and then joined the boys in eating it. The next day, upon visiting this camp, I found everything perfectly quiet and most of the men who were able had gone to their work. Carousals of this kind were a monthly occurrence.

At the end of the year, my contract having expired, I returned to Portland, none the worse for my experience. I then engaged in the baggage and transfer business, which I followed for six years. Tiring of that I became a traveling passenger agent for the Oregon Railroad & Navigation Company, A. L. Maxwell, at the time, being General Passenger Agent. This position I held for five years, and when the great Klondike gold excitement broke out in 1898, I could not resist the temptation of joining the rush, leaving Portland on the first trip of steamer "George W. Elder," which was one of the first to arrive at Skagway, Alaska. At that place I remained for a year, equipping and operating the first bathhouse in Alaska. In this business, I made a large amount of money and sold out for a good figure. I then went to Seattle, Washington.

In the year 1900 the Nome, Alaska, excitement started. Twenty-nine others and myself took passage on a one hundred and fifty ton sailing schooner owned by D. H. Smith and D. Bogan.

On our way to Dutch Harbor, Alaska, my partner, named Jim Harrison, had some misunderstanding with

the captain. On our arrival at Dutch Harbor we found
quite a number of steamships waiting until the ice went
out of the Behring Sea. Wyat Earp had opened a
gambling resort there. Temporarily whiskey was
plentiful. We all enjoyed ourselves, Harrison, meeting
the captain of the schooner, renewed his quarrel and
knocked the captain down. Later I found that the
captains of all the ships in the harbor decided at a
meeting held by them, that none of them would allow
Harrison and myself to travel on any of their ships to
Nome. In other words, they intended to maroon us at
Dutch Harbor. This was not very pleasant news. I,
knowing Captain Tuttle of the Steamer "Bear," appealed to him. He informed me he could fix it for me
to go on any steamer, but I must not associate with
Harrison. This offer I refused and stayed by Harrison. We then received notice from the captain of
the schooner, General McPherson, to come out in a
small boat and remove our effects. This we proceeded
to do. On our arrival at the schooner's side, we found
the captain and first officer standing aft, each with
a six shooter in his hand. I remarked to Harrison,
"Don't say one word to them until I can get into my
room and get my shot gun and put in two cartridges."
We boarded the schooner, the captain and mate looking
daggers at us. I secured the shot gun. Jim began
folding up our blankets. When the captain and mate
came down into the cabin, I stood guard with the shot
gun while Jim packed our belongings. Then I ordered
the captain and mate to step aside and allow us to depart in peace, or I would blow their heads off. They
let us depart in peace. I boarded the small boat,
guarding Jim while he did likewise, and reached the
shore without further trouble. This news was much
exaggerated by the captain and mate. Now came the
trial of getting passage to Nome. I finally found a
steward I had known in Portland, who was employed

on the steam schooner "Nelson." He smuggled both of us on the ship, bringing our belongings by piece meal until all was aboard. We arrived in Nome in good shape, after bucking ice for six days.

In a few days six of us with packs on our backs, started for the interior. On the third day out I concluded that the undertaking was too much for me, and realized that I was too old to stand the **"Hard Knocks"** I had withstood in the past, and turning over my pack to my comrades, after I had retained sufficient goods to last me, I returned to Nome. From Nome I took a steamer to Seattle, Washington, concluding I would pass the remainder of my life where there were paved streets, porcelain bathtubs and beds to sleep in. I did not stay in Seattle, however. After a while I moved to Portland, Oregon.

CHAPTER XXV.

MY BUFFALO VENTURE IN PORTLAND.

JACK RUGG and myself purchased from Howard Eaton two buffalo, one male and one female, for one thousand dollars, delivered at Portland. Eaton at this time owned a large herd of buffalo in Montana. Our contract with him was that the cow should be with calf, as we wished it to be born in Portland. Our intention was to exhibit them. At Calispel, the nearest point, the cow in trying to jump out of the corral, injured herself, causing a premature birth. Eaton wired me what had happened and I instructed him to save the dead calf.

Upon the car's arrival here, I gave the dead calf to L. L. Hawkins, who at that time was gathering relics for the City Museum. The buffalo I transported in a covered dray to a large tent, which enclosed a steel cage sixteen feet square and eight feet high, and in a short time I had tamed the male buffalo by feeding him myself three times a day. He was very fond of wild pea vines. I named him "Joe" and every time I fed him I called him by his name. Learning his name and knowing he was to be fed, Joe became quite gentle, so much so, that I could put my hand on his head. The cow I could not tame. She was frightfully mean and wild, and I could do nothing with her.

Our venture turned out a failure and left us with two buffalo on our hands. After consulting with Mr. Rugg, we concluded to sell them to the city for their parks, which I succeeded in doing, receiving for them seven hundred and fifty dollars. From those two buffalo the city now have a herd of five fine specimens of these noble animals. Old Joe was killed two years ago by his son—they having fought a great battle to the death for the supremacy of the herd. Joe being the older and less able to defend himself, had to succumb to youth and was horribly gored to death. The cow died previously.

I am still residing in Portland, Oregon, and am in fairly good health, and where I hope to remain until I cross the Great Divide.

Should any of my old-time companions visit Portland, I shall be pleased to see them and they will always find the latch string on the outside of my door.

THE END.

INDEX